SNOW ANGELS

BY
CHRISTINE DWYER HICKEY

NEW ISLAND

SNOW ANGELS

First published in 2015
by
New Island Books,
16 Priory Hall Office Park,
Stillorgan,
County Dublin,
Republic of Ireland.

www.newisland.ie

ISBN: 978-1-84840-418-2

British Library Cataloguing Data.
A CIP catalogue record for this book is available from the British
Library.

Typeset by JVR Creative India
Cover photo by Ste Murray (www.ste.ie)
Printed by SPRINT-print Ltd.

New Island received financial assistance from The Arts Council (*An
Chomhairle Ealaíon*), 70 Merrion Square, Dublin 2, Ireland.

10 9 8 7 6 5 4 3 2 1

About the Author

Christine Dwyer Hickey is a novelist and short story writer. Her novel, *The Cold Eye of Heaven* won the Irish Novel of the Year Award in 2012 and was nominated for the IMPAC Award. *Tatty* (2004) was nominated for the Orange Prize and was chosen as one of the 50 Irish Novels of the Decade. *Last Train from Liguria* (2009) was nominated for the Prix Européen de Littérature. Her short story collection, *The House on Parkgate Street and other Dublin Stories* was published by New Island in November 2013. Her seventh novel, *The Lives of Women*, will be published in April 2015 by Atlantic Books.

Snow Angels is her first play and it premiered at the Project Arts Centre in March 2014. She is a member of Aosdána.

Acknowledgements

The Dice Players and the author would like to thank Diego Fasciati and Maureen White of Rough Magic, and Cian O'Brien of The Project Arts Theatre, for all their help in bringing *Snow Angels* to the stage.

The first performance of *Snow Angels* was given at the Project Arts Centre, Dublin on 5th March 2014 by the Dice Players. It was directed by Rosemary McKenna and the stage design was by Cait Corkery. The cast was as follows:

JIM	Des Hickey
OSCAR	Ger Hough
SEBASTIAN	Michael Hough
RABBIT	Oswald

Music by Denis J. Hickey

Snowfall sung by Fiadh Edison

Set in an isolated house, down a lane, at the bottom of a hill, away from the main road, just outside the city centre. Three characters, two of which are brothers from a small country town.

OSCAR (30) – the younger: wiry, tidy, talkative, nervy. Eternal student.

SEBASTIAN (31) – the elder: hot-headed and physically menacing. Recently made redundant from a men's dress hire shop. Has just finished writing his first novel.

JIM (31) – pianist, friend of Oscar's. Irish citizen, but has lived in Germany since he was a small child (4 years old). German accent with hints of Dublin. Slightly more refined, quieter, although appears to be physically robust (half-Russian, but we don't know that yet).

They are all suffering from different types of hangovers. Jim is depressed. Oscar is anxious and hyper. Sebastian is physically hungover.

N.B. Music has an important role to play and is an essential part of the plot.

1. **Snowfall** (instrumental): This is a distorted version of the Snowfall song (including the sound of turning locks and clanking chains), and should indicate fear and bring a nightmare-like quality to the atmosphere. It will play quietly as Jim lies asleep on the floor and the audience comes into the theatre. It will then be used between the scenes. It needs to build up – at first just a few notes, then a few more, scene after scene. Following scenes 6 and 7 there will be a few notes that are sung, i.e. vocals without

3

words by a boy treble. Scene by scene, the song must build into something the audience will be able to recognise when it becomes fully formed towards the end of the final act as:

2. **Snowfall** (song): Piano intro, with the later addition of the voice of a boy treble (vocals without words). In the final scene, words (in German) will be included.

Only JIM (and the audience) will be able to hear any background tracks until the last few minutes. N.B. JIM should also hear the music in his head here and there throughout the play.

Note: a real rabbit must be used. A toy rabbit can be substituted for the fight scene.

The sitting room, furnished cheaply in the way of rented houses. Downstage, i.e. looking out over the audience, a large window is imagined. Downstage Right is a desk and a chair. On the desk is a stack of dictionaries and other books. On the floor Left Centre is a shoebox overflowing with bow ties. Downstage Left Centre is a large box containing miscellaneous clothes and boys' toys (from the 1980s), some of which are visible. A small Christmas tree lies beside this. Pages of balled-up newspapers are strewn about the place; some items are still wrapped in paper. Upstage Right to Right Centre is the kitchen door, through which (Offstage) is the door to the hall, the front door, Sebastian's and Jim's bedrooms and the bathroom. Centre to Downstage Left is a sofa and coffee table. Centre Stage Left is a closed interior door, which leads to Oscar's bedroom. At the side of this door is a haversack overflowing with college books on various subjects. Snow can be seen falling on an overhead projection sheet and/or through a second window Upstage Left. If used, this window will gradually become completely banked up by snow.

SCENE 1

The day after moving in.

In the grey light, JIM *is asleep on the floor. He wears a heavy overcoat over a tuxedo. His left hand is heavily (and clumsily) bandaged; a bow tie is sticking out of the pocket of the overcoat. In his sleep he stirs, his right hand moving as if struggling to play the music on a piano. A distorted version of* **Snowfall** (instrumental) *is playing.*

JIM *wakes with a start, gasping for air. The music abruptly stops. Afraid and confused by his dream, he sits up (getting a painful head-rush). He looks at his bandaged hand, and remembers something from the night before. He stands, and begins hurriedly to unbandage his hand. He stops abruptly when the door to the kitchen opens and he hears* OSCAR *enter the room. He keeps his hand hidden.*

Enter OSCAR. *He is wearing the trousers of a tuxedo, and has a bow tie around his neck. His chest is bare, as are his feet. (He is carrying his shoes in his right hand.) On seeing* JIM *(who has his back to* OSCAR*),* OSCAR *pauses, throws a guilty glance at him, then continues towards the sofa/chair, pushing newspapers out of the way before sitting down.*

(Unless otherwise stated, the two men move around the room [or not] as feels natural during this act, but there should be plenty of movement.)

OSCAR   The mess your man leaves, wha'?

OSCAR *glances at* JIM *now and then. He pulls a sock out of one trouser pocket and puts it on.*

OSCAR   He's not up yet, no?

OSCAR *casts an irritated eye over the mess, then pulls the other sock out of the other pocket and puts that on.*

JIM *(restrained but pointed)* Fuck. Off.

OSCAR   Ooooo, that's lovely. And here was me thinking you Germans had nice manners.

JIM   How many times? I am *Irish.*... Look ... just ... open the door, would you?

OSCAR *lifts one shoe, sniffs the sole and puts it on. He sniffs the second shoe and recoils.*

OSCAR   What door? Here, do you know what happened me on the way back here last night? I stood in shite. There, look, there it is now *(holds the shoe out).*

JIM *(slow, annoyed)* The door to my room? Will you open it? Please?

OSCAR   Open it yourself, why don't ya? No doormen in this house.

JIM   It's *locked.*

OSCAR   Oh...? Well, you needn't be lookin' at me....

Snowfall *piano intro begins playing in* JIM*'s head.*

JIM *(quiet)*   My head, my....

7

Head in hands, he struggles with the music while OSCAR *rambles away to himself.*

OSCAR (*fast delivery*) Is all I'm doin' is tryin' to get a bit of a conversation going, you know? But of course you probably don't know, if last night was anythin' to go by. Don't know what them two girls must have thought. Not a squeak outta you. Skulking off then after five minutes to go drink on your own.

Beat while OSCAR *waits for* JIM *to say something (he doesn't).*

OSCAR A fella could go off his head you know, talkin' to himself. I'd a summer job one time in the local nut shop, and I tell you, most of them's only in there because they'd no one to talk to and had to resort to themselves instead. And sure that'd wear you out. Doin' the work of two, do you see? Maybe even more, say, if the second fella is the sociable sort and invites a crowd back after the pub.

JIM *stands and begins towards* OSCAR.

OSCAR And what if there was a sing-song then? Can you imagine … the racket goin' on inside in your head…? No wonder you'd be a….

JIM I want … the key so I can get my stuff and get the hell *out*. (*Opens his hand for the key.*)

OSCAR And I'm tired tellin' you I don't have any keys. Why, where you goin'?

JIM (*pulls back*) Just … just out.

OSCAR	Now, you said you'd help me with the party, don't forget.
JIM	No, *you* said I'd help you.
OSCAR *(stands)*	Ah, relax why don't you? Sebastian'll have the keys. Look, I've a bit of brekkie put by: half sliced pan, a couple of them little plastic jam yokes. Lifted from the college canteen yesterday. Get it into us quick now before he gets up.
JIM *(snarly)*	I don't want your bit of… *(searches for the word)* 'brekkie'? I want *out*.

JIM *gives him a filthy look and turns his back to him. A few notes of* **Snowfall** (instrumental) *begins.*

OSCAR *(peevish)*	Wasn't me started that fight *(fixes on* JIM*)*. If that's what you're thick about … *(beat)* I say it wasn't me…. Ah look, Jim … you were a child when you left here. It's a different town now, you know. Fights … well, they're a part of life, the drinking life anyhow. And Sebastian? I wouldn't have a word said against him … but, well, he's a bit of a bollix to be honest. *(Beat.)* I said, I didn't start it … are you listenin'?
JIM	I don't *care* about the stupid fight … who started it. I don't *care*. *(With his good hand, he reaches down for a bottle of water on the ground.)*
OSCAR	Well, how come you're not talkin' to me then?

JIM *(noticing the shaking of his own hand)* I *am* talking to you.

OSCAR   Really?

JIM   Yesss. *(He takes a swig from the bottle.)*

OSCAR   When then? Because you've said fuck all so far.

JIM   What do you *want* me to say?

OSCAR *perks up and perches himself on the arm of the sofa.*

OSCAR *(fast delivery)* Oh God, now I'd leave that up to yourself. Whatever'd come into your head. Long as it'd be loquacious like. Do you like that: lo-qua-cious? Got that from your man's thesaurus. I coulda said conversational either. Or chatty even. But sure what would be the point of a thesaurus then…?

JIM   Oh Christ….

OSCAR   Which reminds me *(he starts limping towards haversack of books by the wall),* better put it back before he gets up. Goes mad if you touch his things, by the way *(takes thesaurus out of bag and brings it back to desk),* and here there's plenty other dictionaries too … for the straight talker like, the fella who doesn't mind other people knowin' what he's on about *(arrives at desk, picks up book).* There's even a dictionary of literary terms, if you're more the sort who prefers commentin' through the letterbox on other people's work. Note, it's a *concise* dictionary of literary terms because like you wouldn't want to be wafflin' on when you're talking through your hole on such matters.

JIM *(almost alarmed)* What is this? Are you on coke or something?

OSCAR   Coke? what would I need coke for? *(Beat.)* Sure
                  I'm not even allowed eat orange icepops.

    OSCAR *begins to tidy up dictionaries.*

OSCAR   Must be a million words sat on this desk just
                  waiting to be plucked out and cake-mixed into
                  a novel. Latin! Like who the fuck speaks Latin
                  in the inner city? That's where his novel is set,
                  by the way. The inner city. No, let me correct
                  that. The gritty inner city. Or is that the inner
                  gritty city?

JIM *(absent, nursing headache)* His novel? Oh yeah ... he has that
                  meeting today.

OSCAR   Told you about that, did he?

JIM   I heard him say something....

OSCAR   What? What you hear?

JIM *(a little impatient)* He was just ... I don't know, going on about it.

    JIM *closes his eyes and wearily puts his head back.* OSCAR
    limps Upstage towards the kitchen. JIM *gets a whiff of the shoe*
    as he passes.

JIM   Oh Jesus, the shoe. Put it outside. Put it out!

OSCAR   Can't. Front door's locked.

JIM *(stands)*   Well *open* it, can't you?

OSCAR   It's locked from the inside ... one of those
                  fancy security jobs. Need keeeys, you see.

11

JIM   Well get *keeeeys.*

OSCAR   Sebastian'll have them. You know the way he can get a bit security-conscious when he's been drinking.

JIM   In fact, no. That must be something else you forgot to tell me about him.

OSCAR   Oh yeah. After a real bender he would. The jitters is all it is. Always like that. Slept with the light on, till he was … well, wanking age, I suppose. The dark, you see … gets to him. Ah, don't worry, you'll soon get used to his little ways.

JIM *(almost to self)* I have no intention of getting used to his little ways.

     OSCAR *begins to sort through boxes. He unwraps a cup with no handle.*

OSCAR   Went lookin' for you after last night…?

JIM *(agitated, picks up his phone, shakes it, puts it down, looks at it again)* Do you have a charger?

OSCAR *(stops)*   Important, is it?

JIM *(gestures impatiently)* I just need to cancel … it's nothing.

     OSCAR, *at the desk, lays the shitey shoe on the books.*

OSCAR   Couldn't see you anywhere. What do you need to cancel?

JIM   Are you always this bloody nosey?

Beat while JIM *works up to telling* OSCAR. OSCAR *is playing with the books.*

JIM   Listen, Oscar ... this ... this *(searches for the word)* ... arrangement we have. I'm ... I'm sorry, but ... I don't think this is going to work out.

OSCAR   What are you on about?

JIM   I'm not comfortable here.

OSCAR   Comfortable?

JIM   This house. This area. Everything. I'm not....

OSCAR   What are you on about, comfortable? Know where I ended up sleeping last night? Under the kitchen table is where. Like an oul' dog.

JIM   He locked your room too?

OSCAR   *First* he dragged me up out of me bed, *then* he locked it.

JIM   You see? It is not just the house. It's Sebastian. Quite frankly....

OSCAR   You don't know him yet is all.

JIM   But really, if you think about it ... I don't know you that well either.

OSCAR   All the time we've been knocking around and you say that to me?

JIM   That's just drinking in the same pub, Oscar.

OSCAR   But sure how else would we know each
               other?

JIM   It's not real.

OSCAR   Of course it's real. You're there. I'm there. We
               drink, get drunk, get drunker, see where the night
               takes us....

JIM   It's not real. That's the whole point of it. *Not*
               to be real. I need peace and quiet. Be reason-
               able.

OSCAR   Reasonable?

JIM   I need a night's sleep. I need ... I need to keep
               steady (*glances at his hand again*). All this drinking.
               Noise. Distraction.

OSCAR   But sure the drinking has hardly started yet!

JIM   I'm trying to tell you, I've had enough of it. I'm
               tired. My brain is tired, my bones are tired. My
               hands are tired. I'm so fucking tired, Oscar....
               (*Sits down.*) This place....

OSCAR   I picked this house for your convenience. So
               there'd be room for you and *your* piano, and no
               neighbours to complain about either of ye. If
               it had been down to me, I'd have taken that
               apartment on the quays. Plenty a noise there.
               A pub on the corner. Spar shop underneath.
               Well ... the pub is closed down, but there's the
               Spar. Somewhere there'd have been more of a
               chance of, you know, meetin' a few people, a
               girl maybe.

JIM   In the Spar?

OSCAR   And now here I am, stuck in a poxy bungalow
             all on its own, nothing around but the shell of a
             demolished block of corporation flats. A kip at the
             bottom of a lane that I can't even fit a car down.

JIM   You don't have a car.

OSCAR   Yeah, but say if like … after I qualify, and …
             and that.

JIM   Oscar, really. It is better for me to live
             alone.

OSCAR   After all the trouble I took. And now you're
             just gonna….

JIM   But I would like my deposit back.

OSCAR *begins moving around the room, tidying the crumpled
newspapers, picking them up, flattening them out and folding them.*

OSCAR   You'll have to talk to Sebastian about that.

JIM   I gave the deposit to *you*.

OSCAR   I gave it to him. He's the money man. Wouldn't
             let me near it. Saving up, you see. For a house.
             Always wanted that, you know, his own home,
             with his own fireplace, where he can put his
             Pulitzer and his Booker Prize and his Biggest
             Hairy Bollix in the World trophy. Every spare
             cent? Squirrelled.

JIM   Fine, I'll ask Sebastian.

OSCAR   Do … and good luck with that.

JIM   Oscar, you *have* to give it back.

OSCAR   *Sebastian* will have to….

    JIM *glances around, slightly worried. He looks at his phone again.*

JIM   Your charger?

OSCAR   It's in me room. Sorry now *(a touch insincere)*….
               But you'll stay for the party? You'll do that
               much at least? Be straight with me, don't go
               saying you will if you won't, because it's not
               just a housewarm….

JIM   You already told me a million times.

OSCAR   It's me birthday and all.

OSCAR and JIM *(in unison)* Me thirtieth birthday.

    Short pause while OSCAR *ruminates. We see that he's beginning
    to feel the cold.*

OSCAR   This close to the concert? You haven't a hope
               of findin' anywhere. And you need to be prac-
               tising. Less than a fortnight to go before your
               dayboooo. This is your big chance. Don't go
               fuckin' it up now! *(He moves Centre Stage, and
               begins looking for something.)*

JIM *(shifty, worried)* I thought you said he was getting up?

OSCAR   We'll give him a few minutes, seein' as how he
               has company.

JIM   Company?

OSCAR   Why do you think he dragged me up out of me
               bed? He could hardly bring a woman into his own
               room now could he? It's like a lion's den in there.

JIM   We only moved in yesterday! What woman?

OSCAR *(gestures towards bedroom door)* Would you say she's still in
               there with him? And this is a two-part ques-
               tion, by the way, how come he always gets the
               one with the big knockers?

JIM   You can't mean one of those from last...?
               Which one?

OSCAR   Big Knobs, I told you. Her in the purple
               jumper. The one in the beigey jumper? *She* got
               off with Lofty. Got in the van with him after.

JIM   *Lofty?* Jesus.

OSCAR   I know. It's enough to make you lose all faith
               in womankind. Good luck to her anyway, rum-
               maging through the cobwebs on his scrawny
               arse. Of course, Sebastian thinks Lofty's only
               great because he's a lawyer, and therefore
               knows every fuckin' thing about any fuckin'
               thing. The fact that he's a lawyer that's never
               had a client is neither here nor there. I'll give
               him one thing though: he's no trouble pullin'
               the women. Writes poetry, you see. Women ...
               do love all that shite.

JIM   They must be some poems!

OSCAR   I wouldn't know. They're in Irish ... *(beat)*.
               And here, what about that beardy oul' lad with
               them! Did you ever? *Christ*, what the fuck was
               he on?!

JIM *(distracted)*   What beardy oul' lad?

OSCAR   Sitting there behind the two women like a stone all night. Don't think they knew him or any-thing, and didn't like to ask…. Not a squeak out of him.

JIM   I didn't notice him.

OSCAR   Jaysus, you must be blind. The length of the beard on him, sapping wet it was too. Like a little mankey jumper hangin' out of his chin to dry.

JIM *(shakes his head and shrugs)* No.

OSCAR   *What?* Never took his eyes off *you* the whole time … well, until you snuck off. Left then soon after you. Lofty said he was gay *(laughs)*, and gone out to try an' shift you.

JIM   Oh shut up talking crap. And just get the keys.

OSCAR   I will now…. I invited the two women to me party after.

JIM   *What?*

OSCAR   They couldn't come though *(beat)*, but they're coming to your concert. Oh, they were well impressed when they heard about that.

JIM *(appalled)*   *What? What? WHAT?*

OSCAR   I told them … he mightn't have much to say for himself, but that lad's the greatest concert pianist since Wing Wang or Lang Lang or Langer-on or whatever this is he calls himself. *(Throws a quick look around the room, and begins looking for something.)*

JIM *(stands up)*   You'd no right to ask them. You can go and un-ask them now.

OSCAR   It's a concert, a public event ... you didn't see me smokes, no?

JIM   I don't want them. And ... and stop calling it that.

OSCAR   A public event?

JIM   A concert.

OSCAR *searches for smokes, and throughout the following conversation, roots around the room. He is becoming more and more aware of the cold.*

OSCAR   Well, what'll I call it then?

JIM   I don't know. A gig or something.

OSCAR   A gig? A gig! It'll be the earring and the long leather coat next. Anyway, gig is an awful word. A word for people with more balls than talent.

JIM   I play gigs for a living.

OSCAR   You draw the scratcher for a living.

JIM   What do you think I do in that hotel?

OSCAR   Play muz-ak and melt into the wallpaper. And that's only once a week for a few oul' Americans, who only listen when you play 'Danny Boy'.

JIM   Fuck you! *(He turns away.)*

OSCAR   I must have left them, ah don't tell me I left them. Ah, Jaysus, they're in me room!

OSCAR *takes a lighter out of his pocket and flicks it on and off.*

OSCAR   Which is worse do you think: a light and no
               cigarettes, or cigarettes and no light? *(He
               heats his hands on the lighter, then puts it down on
               the desk.)*

JIM   You'd no right....

OSCAR   Look, in a couple of weeks' time you'll be
               famous, the women'll be flinging themselves
               at you off a catapult.... And I'll be there to
               catch the leftovers. Success, you see, they love
               it. You better get another monkey suit off
               Sebastian. That one you've on is a bit on the
               shabby side.

JIM *(snaps)*   I don't want another awful suit with … with
               the whiff of old vomit and sweat. And, and....

OSCAR   The shadow of a stranger's piss stain, I know,
               I know. But them suits are part of his redun-
               dancy you know, the suits and the miserable
               few quid they threw at him. Anyway, I like
               wearing the suits; makes a night out a bit of
               an occasion. Makes us look very *Ocean's Eleven*,
               actually.

JIM   For a pint on the Inchicore Road? Ridiculous.
               Forget it. Go wake your brother.

OSCAR   I will now in a minute. *(Surveying the room, his eye
               falls on the toy box.)* Still and all, Jim, your room
               couldn't have been locked all night, *(he begins
               towards the box)* I heard you playing.

JIM   What? No you didn't.

OSCAR   Oh God I did. Which way did it go now? La, la, la. *(He begins humming* **Snowfall.***)* La, la, la, la, la, la, la.

JIM *(lifts his head and says, almost to himself)* Impossible!

OSCAR   I heard you, sure. La la la. You could do with a bit more practice on that one....

JIM *(Quietly)*   Impossible....

OSCAR   What's this? A Christmas tree? Look! *(He pulls the tree up, then sits at the box and becomes distracted by the contents, picking up then dropping various toys and Christmas decorations.)* Was this here when we moved in? What is it? Kids' crap. Rubbish.... *(He sticks his hand right down into the bottom of the box and begins tugging at something.)* What's this, what's this? Something woolly. Something warm. Oh, please be a scarf. Even a jumper, please, please, please. *(He pulls out a girl's pink fluffy jumper.)* Shit!

OSCAR *stands up and considers the jumper, then struggles into it. Much too small, the jumper comes to his belly button.*

OSCAR *(minces)*   Well ... what do you think?

JIM *(sharp)*   Suits you.

OSCAR *(lisps)*   Thanks ever so.

JIM   That piece you thought you heard ... which way did it go again?

OSCAR   Eh let's see. No ... gone. Now ... isn't that somethin'? And it turning round and round like a carousel all night in me head.

OSCAR *pulls at the end of his jumper.*

OSCAR   But here … we can wear the suits to your con-
               cert though? *(Beat.)* If we get them dry-cleaned?
               Shirts starched?

JIM   Oscar…? Listen….

OSCAR   I was even thinkin' a buying a proper pair of
               what-you-call-them? Dress shoes.

JIM   Oscar? Listen to me.

OSCAR   Maybe a new bow tie … velvety. You can get
               them in blue you know. Midnight blue, it's called.

JIM   OSCAR! … I can't play.

OSCAR *(slaps him on the back)* Ah, that's just the nerves talkin'.

JIM   I *can't* play *(shows his hand).*

OSCAR   Jesus … what … what happened?

JIM   Sprained.

OSCAR   How? When?

JIM   How do you think? Last night….

OSCAR   The fight? Jesus. That's … I didn't realise. I
               thought you were at the far side of the bar, or
               that you'd gone off someplace else….

JIM   I came back when I heard the row. Tried to
               stop it. I don't know, I maybe stumbled or
               something. Put my hand out anyway, and….

OSCAR	How bad? *(He reaches for the hand.)* Let's see.
JIM	Don't touch it! It hurts. It will be fine. Just that it won't be fine in time.... A few weeks, they said at the hospital.
OSCAR	So that's where you were?
JIM	Half the night in there ... such a place!

Beat while OSCAR *thinks about the fight and Sebastian.*

OSCAR	Sebastian ... bastard. *Bastard.* Aggressive arse-hole. *Arsehole.*
JIM	Look, it wasn't really his fault.
OSCAR	Whose fault was it then? Yours? Mine? The blokes who cracked a few remarks on the shitty dress suits? Whose?
JIM	He didn't *mean....*
OSCAR	He didn't mean? He never means. He never means, but he always, *always....*
JIM	Now look, Oscar. I don't want this turning into a big.... I feel bad enough, you know? Don't mention this to Sebastian, please.
OSCAR	Ah, he's not fuckin' blind. He'll notice....
JIM	Did *you?* Did you notice? Otherwise, I mean it, I'm leaving. Give me your word now you won't say anything.
OSCAR	*What?*

JIM *(stands)*   If you tell him, I'm leaving. I mean it. Give me your word!

OSCAR   Yeah, fine. Okay. Understood…. Under-fuckin'-stood! *(He sits on the sofa and thumps it.)* And I was really looking forward to that concert. Fuck it anyway. Fuck it.…

JIM *comes front of stage and looks out over the audience as if through a window.* **Snowfall** *begins to play.*

JIM   Jesus…. Oscar? Look at this … look.

OSCAR *(sulky)*   Wha'? (OSCAR *gets up and begins reluctantly towards him, until….)* Is that…? Is that…? Ah, you're jokin' me? Ah God, would you look at that! There's enough of it too. How long has that been going on?

JIM   A while … it's obvious.

OSCAR *and* JIM *stand staring out the window for a few seconds. Oscar is childlike and smiling, until:*

OSCAR   Oh God, Jim, your hand … I mean, it's fuckin' terrible, it's just.…

JIM   Forget it. My own fault. One of the first things we learn: never, *ever* put your hands at risk. But would you look at that, *snow.*

OSCAR   Jaysus, you'd get dizzy looking at it after a while, wouldn't you though?

JIM   That's what I like about it.

OSCAR   Gettin' dizzy?

JIM	The way it makes everything … stop. Everything in here *quietens*, and I begin to hear … nothing.
OSCAR	Nothin'?
JIM	Not a thought, not a note.
OSCAR	And that's what you like about it?
JIM	That's what I like about it.

Snowfall *plays.*

OSCAR	Here, do you know what we could do for the party? We could make a snowman. Imagine him, just standing there, greetin' people as they come in. Will we? Build one? A snowman? What do you think?
JIM *(flat)*	Shhh.
OSCAR	One time when we were kids, meself and Sebastian right, we made this snowman. The Patriot Snowman, we called him, and….
JIM	Oscar? Shut up.
OSCAR	Ah no, really, it was just….
JIM *(sharper)*	Shhhh. Just s*hhhh-shhh.*

OSCAR *looks at* JIM, *opens his mouth, then closes it again.*

Fade. End of scene.

SCENE 2

Some time later (ten minutes or so).
From the kitchen we hear the press doors opening and closing.

JIM   All that banging. All that *noise*....

OSCAR   I'm looking for the.... *(Shouts.)* Jaysus! Fuck
                       almighty. Sweet Sufferin' *Christ*, me heart!

JIM   What? What?

OSCAR appears from the kitchen, breathless and half-laughing.

OSCAR   A rabbit.

JIM   A *what?*

OSCAR   A rabbit. I opened the door of the press and
                       there was a rabbit in there at our sliced pan.

JIM   Where? Are you sure? A rabbit?

OSCAR   Leapt out and passed me.

OSCAR goes back into the kitchen and comes back out with a torn slice of
bread and the plastic wrapper.

OSCAR   Little bastard's after ayting all our bread.

JIM   It wasn't a rat now?

OSCAR   It was big and fat and white….

JIM   Yeah…?

OSCAR *(defensive)* I'm not in the deetees, if *that's* what you're implyin'.

JIM   You drink enough.

OSCAR *(comes back out)* Look, a rabbit jumped out of the press.

JIM   Of course he did.

> OSCAR *absentmindedly begins eating the bread as he surveys the room.*

OSCAR   Ah, fuck this. And I can't even text the bastard and tell him get up because me phone is in there with him. Me phone *and* me smokes. *(He keeps looking for the rabbit as he moves towards the bedroom door.)* It's about time. *(He stops and looks behind his haversack.)* And there was a rabbit. *Is* a rabbit, somewhere in this house…. *(He stops short of the bedroom door.)* Jaysus though…. What if … you know?

JIM   What *now?*

OSCAR   He's in there with your one. Oh, they were getting on very well last night, you know.

JIM *(a little worried)* They were…? And what did you talk about? Did you hear?

OSCAR *(absent)*   Naah, one of them deep-down, trespassers-keep-out kinda conversations. *(He starts looking around for the rabbit again.)*

JIM *(quiet)*   Wake your brother up.

OSCAR   Right. I will now. *(He stops.)* Just ... you wouldn't like to be disturbin' a fella if he's....

JIM *(turns to the window, the snow is heavier)* Look at it. Oscar, we need to get those keys.

OSCAR *(buying time)* Yeah. Yeah, I know. *(He pulls up the Christmas tree.)* Will I set this up for the party? What do you think? I will. *(He begins putting the tree together.)* Tell you what though, they were a right pair when you think about it. Sebastian's one ... well, she was rough enough, wasn't she? Where would you say she was from?

JIM   Those flats over there.

OSCAR   Before they were demolished like?

JIM   Obviously.

OSCAR   A right gurrier, if you know what I mean. You know ... like a low type of individual.

JIM   I know what a gurrier means.

OSCAR   I'd say if you got a dig off her you'd know all about it. Here ... how do you know she used to live there? You weren't talkin' to her, were you?

JIM   I used to live down the hall from her.

OSCAR   You did all right now, I'd say. Ha!

JIM   I did. Before I moved to Germany.

OSCAR   Are you serious, Jim?

JIM   Why wouldn't I be?

OSCAR   You just don't seem to be … I mean, not with her sort.

JIM   It was a block of flats, Oscar, not a zoo.

OSCAR   And did she recognise you?

JIM (*a little worried*) I'm not sure.

OSCAR   So your folks, they lived…?

JIM   My mother.

OSCAR   Right. So how come you didn't talk to your woman then?

JIM   Talk?

OSCAR   Yeah, you know, oh, how are you going, long time no see. How's the family been keeping, whatever happened to your man from number thirty-four … that sort of thing.

JIM   *Why?* Why would I want to talk to her? It was years ago, we were kids. I went away to school. My mother moved away after that.

OSCAR   Yeah, but…?

JIM   But what, Oscar? Not everyone needs to talk all the time. Talk just for the sake of it. Always talking. Go wake your brother up. Christ!

OSCAR   All right. Jaysus. I was only asking.

JIM   Well *come on* then.

OSCAR *puts his ear to the bedroom door.*

OSCAR   If he was asleep, there'd be snoring. Although, having said that, he does snore sometimes when he's awake, so....

JIM   You make him sound like such a troll.

Enter SEBASTIAN*, head appearing from around the side of the kitchen area.*

OSCAR   He *is* a fuckin' troll. Yeah, and like if he was havin' sex, we'd be sure to hear him. One time, right, he picked up this one from Liverpool, over for a hen party. I should say the Liverpool one picked him up.

SEBASTIAN *slowly begins to move from the kitchen area towards the two at the door. He's wearing a dress shirt, socks and no trousers. He is carrying the rabbit in his arms.*

OSCAR   You could hear *everything. Every-fuckin'-thing.*

JIM   Oh please, I don't need to know.

OSCAR   Oh yeah, oh yeah, more, more, oh yeah, hmmm, oh that's nice. Oh yeah, lower, higher, round the corner there and next turn on the left, stop when you come to the T-junction. Loverly.

JIM *starts to laugh despite himself.*

OSCAR   And the carry-on of him for fuck sake was even worse, howling he was. Howling, I'm telling you. He howls.

JIM   What, like a tom cat?

OSCAR   More like a wolf, I'd say.

JIM   Like a...? *(He starts laughing.)* You mean like ... Aoooo. *(He quietly makes a howling noise. Both are trying not to laugh out loud.)*

OSCAR   No it was more, owwwuuuuuuh.

JIM   You mean....

SEBASTIAN, *now behind them, throws back his head and lets out a long howl.*

SEBASTIAN   ARRRRROOOOWWWowowwow.

OSCAR *and* JIM *both jump.*

OSCAR   Jesus, Sebastian! Me heart for fuck's sake.

Centre Stage, SEBASTIAN *glares at* OSCAR.

Throughout this scene he avoids looking directly at JIM, *even when addressing him.* JIM, *standing Centre Left, is also a little wary of Sebastian.* OSCAR *makes several attempts to caress the rabbit.* SEBASTIAN *slaps his hand away each time. He shows great affection for the rabbit. Addressing it, caressing it, etc.*

SEBASTIAN   Tellin' my private business to strangers?

OSCAR   He's hardly a stranger. Where did you get…?

SEBASTIAN   He is to me. Who's in the jacks?

OSCAR *(to* JIM*)* Told you there was a rabbit! *(To* SEBASTIAN*)*
                 Where did…?

SEBASTIAN   I found him in the hall. Now who's in the…?

OSCAR   There's no one in the jacks. *(To* JIM*)* Told ya!
                 Told ya! *(To* RABBIT*)* Hello, Rabbit … do you
                 remember me, doya?

SEBASTIAN   Who's in the jacks? I'm askin'….

OSCAR   And I'm tellin' you, there's no one. Unless you
                 brought…?

SEBASTIAN   I brought no one back. Right. Play your little
                 games. Just gimme me key so. *(He puts one hand
                 out to* JIM.*)*

JIM   There is no key. Only a bolt.…

SEBASTIAN *(getting more annoyed)* I'm not talking about the key to the
                 jacks, I'm talking about the key to me bedroom.

JIM   Don't say that's locked too?

SEBASTIAN   Why else now would I be lookin' for the key?

JIM   But I thought … did you not? Take all the keys?

SEBASTIAN   What are you on about? *(To* OSCAR*)* What's
                 he on about?

OSCAR   Nawthin'.

SEBASTIAN   *(Sneers)* Naaawwthin'. Telling his little fib-
                     bers again, was he? *(He reaches out and plucks*
                     OSCAR*'s face.)*

OSCAR   Oww! Get off, you.

SEBASTIAN   I got up to go to the jacks in the middle of the
                     night. The jacks was locked. So I went back to
                     my room. And guess what?

OSCAR   It was locked.

SEBASTIAN   And people think accountants are thick.

JIM   So where did you sleep then?

SEBASTIAN   Under the rug in the hall.

OSCAR   I'm not an accountant!

SEBASTIAN   You will be. Then you'll be even thicker.

OSCAR   I'm not even studying accountancy any more, I
                     switched, remember?

SEBASTIAN   You *switched?*

OSCAR   Yeah. Ages ago. Before I started computer
                     studies, and ... after I ... And now I'm....
                     Where did you go to the jacks?

SEBASTIAN   There's a bin in the hall.

OSCAR   Ah Jesus, Sebastian....

SEBASTIAN   What was I supposed to do, tie a knot in it? *(Overcome by the hangover, he goes to the sofa and sits down.)* Have you any headache tablets, have ya?

OSCAR   In me room.

SEBASTIAN   Get a couple there, will ya?

OSCAR   We thought the door was locked, that you were in there....

SEBASTIAN   Well, I'm not, am I? Did you even try the handle? *(A beat while he looks from one to the other.)* All right, girls, hold onto your knickers, I'll do it. *(He goes to the door.)* Anyone in there? *(He bangs again.)* Answer me. Answer me now, or the door won't be the only thing I'll be kickin' in. *(Beat.)* It's locked all right.

SEBASTIAN *moves away from the door and sits on the sofa.*

SEBASTIAN   Have your little joke with your little pal, Oscar. Let me know now when you've finished giggling. *(He closes his eyes.)*

OSCAR   I didn't. We didn't.

SEBASTIAN   Somebody is acting the bollix, and it ain't me.

JIM *goes back to the armchair, hand in pocket, and sits down. He worries.*

OSCAR   Would it be Lofty, playin' some kind of a trick? Maybe showing off in front of your one?

SEBASTIAN   Your one?

OSCAR   From last night. Your one who got in the van
                 with him after.

SEBASTIAN   Did she now? Come on the Loft! Which your-
                 one was that?

OSCAR   Not your one with the purple jumper, the other
                 with the....

SEBASTIAN   Not everyone has a thing for women's jumpers,
                 you know. I see you've even taken to wearin'
                 them yourself now.

OSCAR *(embarrassed, pulls at his jumper)* We thought she was in
                 there with you....

SEBASTIAN   Lorraine?

OSCAR   Is that her name? Jim used to know her.

SEBASTIAN   Oh, I know he used to know her. *(Pointedly.)* And
                 do you know how I know that? She told me.

*SEBASTIAN stays on the sofa with the rabbit. His breathing
is laboured.*

OSCAR   So what'll we do?

SEBASTIAN   About wha'?

OSCAR   About what!? We're locked into the house,
                 there's not a crumb in. We're supposed to be
                 throwin' a party tonight. It's snowin'. And I'm
                 starvin' by the way....

SEBASTIAN   Relax, willya? Lofty will be here soon.

OSCAR   *And?*

SEBASTIAN   Jesus, Oscar. Me head's fuckin' burstin' over here.

OSCAR   The front door? You need the security key to open it....

SEBASTIAN   Yeah?

OSCAR   So what's he goin' to do then, write a fuckin' poem to it?

SEBASTIAN (*vague*) Ahh, he'll think of something. Kick it in, if he has to.

OSCAR   Oh God, I was forgettin' about Super Lofty there for a minute. He weighs about three stone. Stupid oul' fella can hardly walk with the piles, never mind kick in a solid front door.

SEBASTIAN (*getting annoyed*) Look, he'll be here.

OSCAR   Well can't you phone him or somethin', tell him hurry?

SEBASTIAN   Oh, that's a brilliant idea, Oscar. Now why didn't I think of that?

SEBASTIAN *stands up, looks down the front of his under-pants, then begins patting around his backside as if searching for something.* JIM *opens his eyes.*

SEBASTIAN   Do you know what it is? Didn't I forget to stick me phone up me arse?

OSCAR   *What?*

SEBASTIAN	Like, where else would it beeeee? *(He sits back down.)* Now shut up will ya? He said he'll be here, he'll be here.
OSCAR	Oh yeah, like he said he'd give you a lift to the supermarket yesterday.
SEBASTIAN	He's doing that today. But first he's giving me a lift to the publishers. Very supportive that way, is Lofty. More than I can say for some pink, fluffy, begrudgin' bastards around here. Not mentionin' any names.
OSCAR	The publishers…?
SEBASTIAN	Don't say you forgot? Don't say you let it slip your jealous little mind…?
OSCAR	No. I just wasn't sure of the day….
SEBASTIAN	Who knows, we might even have something to celebrate after, wha'? *(He nuzzles the rabbit.)*

JIM *looks on while the two brothers begin to argue.*

OSCAR *(overkeen)*	Better…. Better go the supermarket first. I mean *before* the publishers.
SEBASTIAN	Ah, what difference?
OSCAR	No, no, no. See if you bring the stuff back here first. Get it over with and that. Me and Jim, we can, you know, be settin' the party up and that. And you can go for a drink with Lofty. And anyway, with the snow and that, they might, you know, run out of stuff….

37

SEBASTIAN   And that… *(beat)*. You forgot to say 'and that'. What the fuck is up with you? What are you being so twitchy about? He's very twitchy, isn't he? *(To* RABBIT*)* Even twitchier than you.

OSCAR   Ah, I just wanna make sure….

SEBASTIAN   Look, It'll all depend on Lofty's schedule.

OSCAR   Lofty's schedule? *Lofty's?* Since when did…? *(Pulls back.)* Yeah. Okay. I just think you should. First, because….

SEBASTIAN   Will you shut up, Oscar, you're like an oul' one there goin' on about the blaydin' supermarket.

JIM   I have a question … the keys? If Sebastian doesn't have them, then…?

SEBASTIAN   Oh.

JIM   'Oh'?

SEBASTIAN   Oh Fuck.

OSCAR   What?

SEBASTIAN   The front door mat….

OSCAR *goes to move in the direction of the front door.*

SEBASTIAN   The *far* side of the door, ya thick ya … the front step mat, where we agreed to leave them for each other. We never got round to getting the spare sets cut.

OSCAR   You mean *you* never got round to gettin' the spare keys cut.

SEBASTIAN   I'm doin' it today.

OSCAR   Oh yeah, you're doin' a lot today. Today is a big day all right, Sebastian. And how is it workin' out for you so far? Sittin' in your khaks on the sofa playin' with a fuckin' bunny rabbit. What about me party? I've people comin' to me party!

SEBASTIAN   Now, now, Oscar. Take it easy, old boy. You know what happens when you get overexcited. *(He lies back and lifts the rabbit up over his head.)* He's not supposed to get overexcited, you know. 'Overwrung', as Ma-Maa calls it. *(To* OSCAR*)* When I came back last night, the front door was wide open, so I left them there under the mat.

OSCAR   You didn't pick them up? You didn't bother your boll…?

SEBASTIAN   Why would I? Maybe it's not locked, maybe it just got jammed or something.

JIM   It's locked. I already checked. More than once.

OSCAR   Are you sure you saw them there? You didn't have one of your blackouts and forget, now did you?

SEBASTIAN   I'm telling you…. And shut up you about blackouts. That was only once!

OSCAR   Ha!

JIM   So. Okay. Fine. You definitely saw them?

SEBASTIAN   Yesss.

JIM   That's where they are then. Under the mat. Now what?

SEBASTIAN   Well, when Lofty gets here, all he has to do is put them through the letter box and then we open all doors, quick shower and ... I'll head off with him to the publish....

OSCAR   Ah no, first the super....

SEBASTIAN   All right, Jaysus! If there's enough time. I've to have a shower first. And iron a shirt. Do you think I should have the shirt ironed, or would it be more writerly to go a bit crumpled?

JIM   Eh, hold on.

SEBASTIAN   Do we even have an iron?

OSCAR   The shopping is supposed to be *your* job. You said if *we* cleaned the house and moved all the stuff in, *you'd* do the shopping and get the keys cut.

SEBASTIAN   Yeah well, that plan didn't work out, Oscar, did it?

OSCAR   You said, if we ... you said.

JIM   Please. Hold on one moment, I don't....

SEBASTIAN   '*You said.*' '*You said ...*'.

JIM   Hold *on*.

JIM, *with increasing frustration, watches the argument bounce between the two brothers.*

OSCAR   I'm starvin'. Look at me, I'm shakin' with the
               cold. How come you're not cold?

SEBASTIAN   I'm boiling from the drink.

OSCAR   I actually feel a bit weak … like I might be
               gonna faint or something. *(Sits down.)* Wonder
               would I be getting diabetes?

SEBASTIAN   You don't get diabetes just because you missed
               one breakfast.

OSCAR   Didn't Granda' get it, sudden like?

SEBASTIAN   He was 85!

JIM *(comes back in)* There is no … letterbox.

OSCAR   All these *blobs* in front of my eyes. It's the hun-
               ger. My blood sugar is dropped down to me
               toes. You can see me ribs. Look.

SEBASTIAN   Jesus Christ, you'd think you were Bobby
               Sands….

OSCAR   Bobby Sands had a choice at least. Bobby
               Sands had a motive.

SEBASTIAN   A *motive?* What are you talkin' about a motive?!

OSCAR   I'm starving for no reason *and* could be gettin'
               diabetes, all because you couldn't a been arsed
               get the keys cut.

SEBASTIAN   I said I'd get them done today, I'll….

JIM   There. Is. No. Letterbox.

OSCAR   No you won't, you know you won't, you....

SEBASTIAN *(sits up)* I swear I'll plant you now in a minute if you don't shut....

JIM *(vicious)*   *There is no fucking letterbox!*

> SEBASTIAN *and* OSCAR *start. They look at* JIM, *then exchange a glance.*

SEBASTIAN   All right. Jaysus....

(Beat.)

OSCAR   Sure how else would we get letters?

JIM   *Think* about it.

OSCAR   He's right. There's a sort of steel plate over the door....

JIM   And something else ... there's no back door in this house.

SEBASTIAN   So what? There's no stairs either. Wooo-ooo. Big thrill.

OSCAR   That's because it's a bungalow.

JIM   With no back door. And bars on the window.

OSCAR   And a front door that's been steel plated. Why? It's not as if there's anyone around to break in.

SEBASTIAN   Yeah, but when you think about it, at some point, someone living in this house was afraid of that front door getting kicked in. Quick, where's me notebook?

SEBASTIAN, *all excited, gets up and looks around for somewhere to put the rabbit. He empties the toy box, and puts a cushion from the sofa into it before putting the rabbit in.*

SEBASTIAN You go a beepy there now like a good bunny bun. Daddy's got work to do.

SEBASTIAN *goes to the desk, takes a hardback notebook from the pile (pen inside) and begins to write.*

JIM No letterbox means no place for Lofty to put the keys.

SEBASTIAN *(gleeful)* I tell you this is a right rough area.... Like that row last night ... that coulda turned nasty, you know? One of us coulda gotten our throats slit. And do you know what your one Lorraine was tellin' me about the what-ya-call-them, them green lumps in the ground? *(He sniffs the air, i.e. shitey shoe.)*

OSCAR Lumps?

SEBASTIAN Yeah, you know, the melted plastic things stuck into the ground ... there's a few as you go up the lane. Kinda clumps. *(Sniffs again.)* The green bins. The kids burn them. For a hit.

OSCAR Clumps? Lumps? What are ye talkin' about?

JIM They steal the bins, set fire to them and inhale the fumes.

SEBASTIAN *(writes in his notebook)* They stand around the burning bin sucking in vapours. *(Looks up.)* Jaysus, there's the first line of the sequel anyway. Lofty says it's as well let them think you've a second one up the sleeve. For the negotiations like … don't want them thinkin' I'm a once-off wonder.

OSCAR   Can we stick to the matter in hand, *please?* The keys? No letterbox? Lofty?

SEBASTIAN   Ah, can't he put them through the window there? *(Sniffs again.)* What is that *smell?*

JIM   That's a plate glass window. You can't open it.

SEBASTIAN   The kitchen window then.

JIM   Yes. But to get to the kitchen window, he would need to scale the back wall. Which is about this high *(lifts his hand to show a height much taller than he is).*

SEBASTIAN   Well, I'm sure if….

OSCAR   Please don't say he could get over that wall.

SEBASTIAN   All I'm saying is, *if*….

OSCAR   I don't believe what I'm hearing.

SEBASTIAN *(large)* I haven't even said it yet.

OSCAR   The shite you come out with.

SEBASTIAN *(half-stands)* The shite I come out with? *I* come out with? What are you deaf now, you can't hear yourself speak? *(He picks up the shoe, sniffs it and looks at it, then looks at the dictionaries.)* Were you at my stuff again?

OSCAR   Lofty? Lofty? Don't make me laugh! Half the time he needs a leg up to get on a bar stool.

SEBASTIAN *begins messing up the dictionaries, i.e. putting the desk back into disorder. He picks up the shoe, smells it and recoils.*

SEBASTIAN   He still managed to get the leg over last night, didn't he? More than you two did. How long has it been, Oscar? And your pal here seems to clam up at the sight of a woman. This keeps up and yez'll have to take to ridin' each other.

JIM *(cringes)*   Jesus! What sort of a ...? You disgust me. *(He turns away in disgust.)*

SEBASTIAN *(to* OSCAR*)* Oh sorry now, I appear to have insulted your friend's sensibilities. *(He puts on the gombeen act.)* I do be forgetting my manners. I do be forgetting what a carefully brought up gent he is, *my arse!*

OSCAR   Ah leave him out of it, can't ye?

SEBASTIAN   And you leave your shitty shoe and snivelly nose out of my business.

SEBASTIAN *stands, and the two brothers edge towards each other.*

SEBASTIAN   Over here poochin' around for a few crumbs to feed your own half-starved excuse of a life, scratching away there, in its rat-hole....

OSCAR   Why don't you just shut the fuck up?

SEBASTIAN   And why don't you fuck the fuck off, and take your shite-encrusted shoe with you.

SEBASTIAN *fires the shoe at* OSCAR.

45

OSCAR There's somethin' wrong with you, do you know that? Somethin' not quite....

SEBASTIAN With me, Oscar? Somethin' wrong with me? Jaysus, that's a good one all right, comin' from you.

OSCAR You big heap a useless shite....

SEBASTIAN Keep it up now. Keep it up....

JIM *(bangs his fist off the wall) Christ!* Stop it. Stop it, you fucking idiots, you stupid fucking idiots. Are you always like this?

SEBASTIAN *(beat while he pulls himself together)* Like what? What's it to do with you what we are or aren't like?

JIM Nothing. Absolutely nothing at all.

(Beat.)

SEBASTIAN We're family, you know? Not that you'd give a fuck about anything like family of course. *(He begins pacing.)* Heard some very interesting things about you last night, I did. Oh yeah, I have the measure of you now all right. Goin' on like you're some sort of somebody with your private school and your German this and that and that accent on ya!

JIM I never claimed to be German. I went to school there, sure. I lived there. Not my choice. I was only a small boy. But I was born *here*. Ah, fuck this, I don't have to explain myself to you.

SEBASTIAN Do you know where he's actually from, Oscar haw? Lord Von Ask-Me-Arse here. He's from them flats down the way. That's how she knows him.

OSCAR *(quiet)*   I know he is. He told me already. Jesus, Sebastian, I never knew you were such a snob.

(Beat.)

SEBASTIAN *(embarrassed)* Yeah, well. Maybe he told you that much, but I bet he didn't tell you … all. I bet….

JIM *(going towards kitchen)* I'm kickin' my bedroom door in, getting my stuff, and leaving through the bedroom window.

OSCAR   But what about your piano, Jim? You don't want to go leaving without your….

JIM *(stops)*   The piano isn't here. I've been trying to tell you!

SEBASTIAN   You fuckin' liar, and you bangin' away on it half the night.

JIM   I wasn't banging on anything.

SEBASTIAN   I heard you. Kept me awake with your banging.

JIM   Look, I wasn't … ah, forget it.

OSCAR *(hesitant)* I'd say that was probably a radio, Sebastian. I heard it too, and I'd say it was….

SEBASTIAN   What radio! *Where?*

JIM   I'm leaving.

SEBASTIAN   Yeah. You do that, go on.

OSCAR   Ah, Jaysus, hold on now, Jim. *Jim?*

SEBASTIAN   Ah, let him go. Go on to fuck.

OSCAR   Always have to be like that with my friends.

SEBASTIAN   Is that what you call him? A friend? What do you know about him, Oscar?

   JIM *disappears into the kitchen.*

OSCAR   He's my friend. And you just can't bear the idea of it.

SEBASTIAN *(jeering)* 'He's my friend.' 'He's my …'. What do you know about him?

OSCAR   That's a stupid question.

SEBASTIAN   Only because you haven't got an answer for it.

   JIM *comes back in, and looks from one to another.*

JIM   It's locked.

OSCAR   Wha'?

JIM   The door to the hall, it is locked.

SEBASTIAN   How could it be? I only walked through it a while ago.

OSCAR   The door *into* the hall, do you mean?

JIM   The door from the kitchen. Into the hall. It is. Fucking. *Locked.*

   SEBASTIAN *goes out through the kitchen. We hear him try the door.*

SEBASTIAN *(Offstage)* It's locked all right. *(He comes back in.)* How could it be locked?

48

OSCAR *(to* SEBASTIAN*)* You think you're funny? Locking all the doors?

SEBASTIAN   *Me?* Ah, come on now.

OSCAR   You and Lofty trying to mess with our heads?

SEBASTIAN   I'm tellin' you, it's got nothin'....

OSCAR   Oh yeah, I can just see it now, Lofty coming back here last night with your one, looking for drink or a place to shag because he still lives with his mother. But sure that's grand, he's only 45 years old.

SEBASTIAN   Will you stop blamin' Lofty on everything?

OSCAR   Lofty comin' in here with his pile-stuffed arse....

SEBASTIAN   You take an unhealthy interest in Lofty's arse if you ask me.

OSCAR   He came in. You were probably still up. And between ye, the plan was concocted....

SEBASTIAN *(large)* And what about *him? (points to* JIM*)*. He's just been out there, he coulda locked the door this minute. But of course you'd rather it was me, wouldn't you?

OSCAR   Don't give me that. Don't give me....

SEBASTIAN   The times *I've* stuck up for *you*, stood between you and....

OSCAR   I never asked! I never asked!

JIM gives *up. His head is hurting, and we see that he is becoming more worried. A few notes of* **Snowfall** *play in his head.*

OSCAR   First you go dragging me out of me bed....

SEBASTIAN   I did in....

OSCAR   ... pushin' me out that door and lockin' it behind me....

SEBASTIAN   I did in my....

OSCAR   Out of me own bed.

SEBASTIAN   Bollix.... You were probably sleepwalking, like you used to do when you were small.

OSCAR   I *was* not. I *did* not....

SEBASTIAN   In the bed with them every night. Oscar the human condom. No wonder the old man couldn't stand you.

OSCAR *(makes a run for him)* You bastard. I'll kill you.

SEBASTIAN *(turns him and lifts him)* Still the same little baba Ossie, still the same....

OSCAR   I'm not. I'm not. I'm....

SEBASTIAN *(slaps him on the arse)* MAMMMEEEE! MAMEEE!

End of Scene

Scene 3

Twenty minutes or so later.
Lights go up (slightly lower than before).

JIM *is at the front window, staring at the snow.* **Snowfall**
(instrumental) *is playing in his head. He is worried, but trying
not to show it.*
OSCAR *is rubbing his belly up against the radiator.*
SEBASTIAN *is half-asleep on the sofa, the box with the rabbit
in it beside him on the floor, his hand protectively holding the side
of it.*

SEBASTIAN *(raises himself)* What time is it anyway?

JIM   I heard the Angelus bells.

SEBASTIAN *(lies down again)* That's not too bad then. Still have
                 a bit of time.

JIM   It was ages ago.

SEBASTIAN   Well, what the fuck are you tellin' me for?

OSCAR   The heatin'. It's nearly gone off. On all night,
                 and now it's….

SEBASTIAN   I turned it off earlier.

OSCAR   What you do that for?

SEBASTIAN   It costs money you know, non-stop heatin'.

OSCAR   Where's the switch?

SEBASTIAN   Hot press.

OSCAR   Where's the…?

SEBASTIAN   Hall.

OSCAR   Scabby bastard. *(He throws his dickie bow at him as he begins towards the front window and joins Jim.)*

SEBASTIAN *(to* JIM*)* How long ago was it you heard them, the bells?

JIM   A while.

SEBASTIAN *(sits up)* What's that mean? A while? How big a while?

OSCAR, *worried, glances at* SEBASTIAN.

OSCAR *(is overly keen. He goes to the sofa and sits down)* Ah, it wasn't that long ago. Relax, you've loads of time. Here, do you know what I was telling Jim there earlier? About the snowman we made when we were kids? Remember Sebastian, the Patriot Snowman? Ah, you shoulda seen him, Jim. A big fat bastard he was and all.

Snowfall *will fade as* JIM *gets drawn into the story.*

OSCAR   We built him on the path out on Main Street. And there was the two of us going down all the doors looking for his gear. Woulda been about 6 and 7 at the time. No front teeth. All cutie-cutie in our duffle coats.

SEBASTIAN *(begins to sit up)* Well, I was. Oscar, much as he is today, was an ugly little bollix.

OSCAR   Anyway, the publican, Ferriter....

SEBASTIAN *Mrs* Ferriter. It was his wife. She gave....

OSCAR   I'm telling it.

SEBASTIAN His wife, Mrs Ferriter, gave us a hat someone had left on a hook. You could scrape the grease off the inside of it with your fingernail.

OSCAR   And a drunken oul' lad up at the bar gave us his pipe....

SEBASTIAN Still wet with his dribbles.

OSCAR   I was gonna say that! About the dribbles. We got a few pebbles a coal from Mr Taylor's depot....

SEBASTIAN No, no. Wrong again. Miserable bastard wouldn't give us any. His wife made some crack about beggars.

OSCAR   Yeah, well anyway.

SEBASTIAN Once a beggar, always....

OSCAR   The snow was so high off the ground....

SEBASTIAN   The English one, she gave us the coal. And bis-
             cuits. Remember her, Oscar? The one with all
             the black stuff on her eyes? Used to sit behind
             the door of Ferriter's lounge. Four gins in, and
             she'd start insulting the customers.

OSCAR   Oh yeah. You'd often see her crying then in the
             window after. Black tears squirting out of her
             eyes, like she'd ink inside in her head.

SEBASTIAN *(jealous of his use of words)* Stick to the story now,
             stick to the….

OSCAR   Mrs Tobin from the greengrocers told us take
             our pick of the carrots.

SEBASTIAN *(guffaws)* Oh Jaysus, this is the best bit. Wait'll you
             hear this! *(He looks at* JIM, *friendly for an instant,
             before pulling himself back.)* The carrots. I forgot
             about the carrots.

OSCAR   Let me tell it, let me tell it … for his nose. Of
             course, we were arguing about which carrot to
             take, so she gave us two, a small one and a big
             one, and told us try both on his face, see which
             suited him best. We still couldn't decide, so in
             the end we used the small one for his nose and
             the big one….

SEBASTIAN *(stands)* For his mickey.

OSCAR *(shouts)*   Mickey! Ah, it's hard to explain, but it was the
             funniest…. Ah, God *(laughter fades).*

SEBASTIAN   Yeah, until we got battered.

JIM   Who battered you?

SEBASTIAN   Who didn't? First our granny, then our mother.
               We let the family down, you see. Then Mrs
               Cassin had a go. She owned the newsagents.

JIM   But why did she...?

OSCAR   See, she'd given us one of those little Irish
               tricolour flags ... you know, the Paddy's Day
               ones made in China? And because our fella was
               outside her shop, facing the street traffic, the
               cars going by beeped at him, and she waving
               out, all delighted with herself and the patriot
               snowman with her tricolour stuck to his chest.

SEBASTIAN   Not dreamin' of course that it was his big orange
               mickey that was attracting all the attention.

OSCAR *and* SEBASTIAN *laugh again.*

OSCAR   In them days it was acceptable for any woman to
               chastise any child really. O yeah, an oul' one'd be
               passing by and go: 'Come here to me, you, I heard
               you gave cheek to your mother last week you little
               bastard, here's a kick up the hole for yourself ...'.

OSCAR *kicks* SEBASTIAN *on the arse.* SEBASTIAN
*glares at him for a second, then decides to let it go and begins to
lope across the floor, Quasimodo-style, towards the window.*

SEBASTIAN   Never done us a bit a harm.

SEBASTIAN *stops at the window, is startled by the amount of
snow. A beat while the three stare out morosely.*

OSCAR   People mind their own business now. Me ma
               would say that's what has the jails full, 'no bud
               nippin',' she'd say.

SEBASTIAN (*quiet but pointed*) Yeah well, she would say that.

OSCAR   But when we were kids....

SEBASTIAN   We were punchbags, so to speak.

OSCAR   I wouldn't go that far now.

SEBASTIAN   You'd be put in jail for the half of it nowadays.

OSCAR (*starts rubbing his belly*) Ah, don't start, you.

SEBASTIAN   All I'm saying is....

> OSCAR *gets a bit agitated and begins to walk around, tidying up. Jim moves away from the window and sits on the side of the sofa, embarrassed.*

OSCAR   Jesus, all we were doing was telling a funny story....

SEBASTIAN   Only tellin' it like it was, that's all. (*He wanders back to the sofa, and picks up his notebook.*)

OSCAR (*comes back to* SEBASTIAN*)* Have to choke the good out of everythin', you.

SEBASTIAN   You know as well as I....

OSCAR   Ah go on then, put it in your notebook. We don't want to hear it. We don't wanna hear it....

SEBASTIAN   Yeah, or shove it under the carpet, Oscar. We don't wanna see it.

OSCAR   In your notebook. Dig it in there, with your poison pen.

SEBASTIAN   Why ... do you think I haven't done that already?

SEBASTIAN *pokes him with the notebook,* OSCAR *pushes it onto the ground.*

OSCAR   Always have to sour everything. With your bile. Take the good out of it. *(He walks away.)* With your bile ... your bitter bile.

JIM *stands,* **Snowfall** (instrumental) *plays. He comes back to the window.* SEBASTIAN *slowly picks up his notebook.*

JIM   I have never seen anything quite like this. Even in Germany. One winter there it snowed and snowed, but nothing like this.

End of scene.

Scene 4

An hour or so later.
Lights up, slightly dimmer than before.

SEBASTIAN *sits with his head back on one end of the sofa, the box with the rabbit in it on his lap.* JIM *sits at the far end of the sofa, on the edge.* OSCAR *has opened the Christmas tree and has brought it Downstage Left Centre. The box of dickie bows is upended, and he's tying dickie bows to the branches.*

OSCAR   What if people turn up?

JIM   *Who?* Who would turn up in this?

OSCAR *(childish)* These two Polish blokes in my class could. Snow'd be nothing to them. And there's this Lithuanian girl. She makes….

JIM   Look at it, Oscar!

OSCAR   … cakes. She might make a cake for … I kinda fancy her, I do. Well, not really. But I feel she'd be approachable, anyhow. I could ask her out, and she wouldn't … *(beat)*. Because some of them, you feel you have to leave your CV in then wait for permission to approach the bench. And then they still tell you piss off.

SEBASTIAN   I'm tired tellin' you, stand still and they'll come to you.

OSCAR   Easy say that.

SEBASTIAN   Ah, you'll always get some oul' slapper at the end of the night who's after spending hours getting done up and doesn't want to waste it.... What time would you say it is now?

OSCAR   I don't want an oul' slapper, I want a girlfriend. Grand if she happens to *be* a slapper....

SEBASTIAN   Shut up, Oscar, will ya? I'm tryin' to think. Jaysus, I could do with a drink.

OSCAR   I don't want one of them ambitious, pushy ones either. Always gone like a hare out of the trap next day. Or worse, bring you back to theirs, and next morning can't wait to get rid of you.

SEBASTIAN *(to* JIM*)* What time would you say it is?

OSCAR   And you do feel like shit then, sitting on your own on the top of the bus, first thing on a Sunday morning, looking down on the lonely streets.

A mobile phone begins to ring Offstage. They listen.

SEBASTIAN *(worried)* Lofty probably.... *(To* JIM*)* Supposin' he can't get the van down the lane? Supposin' he's stuck up there this minute, and we don't even know? What time is it now?

JIM   My phone is dead.

SEBASTIAN *(annoyed)* Have you no watch? How do you tell the time then?

JIM   How do *you*?

SEBASTIAN *(stands and begins to pace)* If I've to *craaawl* through that snow....

    SEBASTIAN *picks up the half bottle of water from the armchair, slugs thirstily from it, then wipes the palm of his hand off the top of the bottle.*

OSCAR   That's not yours. That's Jim's.

SEBASTIAN   I'll fill it up again in a minute.

    SEBASTIAN *wipes the top of the bottle with his hand, then offers the bottle to* JIM, *who refuses.*

SEBASTIAN *(half to himself)* Say it's about ... two or so ... and taking account of driving conditions ... so if I've to be there at five.... *(He takes another quick slug, emptying the bottle, belches softly, and then throws it onto the armchair.)* Isn't that right, Oscar? Five, they said?

OSCAR   Who?

SEBASTIAN   The publishers?

OSCAR   Oh, yeah.

    SEBASTIAN *comes back to the sofa and sits in the narrow space on the far side of* JIM. *During the following conversation he is slightly defensive as he explains to* JIM *(almost as if he's convincing himself). Sitting together,* JIM *edges away from* SEBASTIAN, *who edges after* JIM.

SEBASTIAN   Yeah, meeting them in the Shelbourne. The hotel I mean. Not the ... not the dog track. Lofty was sayin' they probably want to bring me for dinner. He said it's a good sign, anyway ... the Shelbourne. Publish some very good stuff they do ... small company, but respectable. *Respected*, I should say. Just what I want.

JIM   Good, yeah.

SEBASTIAN   You see, my priority wouldn't be commercial. It might sound as if I'm a bit up me own arse, but ... well, I set out to write a work of art. And I want it treated like that. Not like a tin of fuckin' beans on a shelf, you know?

JIM   Sure, yeah.

SEBASTIAN   And do you know what I really liked about them? They've manners, not like some. I approached a few publishers you know, and most of them didn't even reply. Yeah, unbelievable, I know. But this crowd now, they went to the trouble of phoning. The *landline*. Oh yeah, in our old place. Old-fashioned courtesy, I like that. Isn't that right, Oscar?

OSCAR   What?

SEBASTIAN   They phoned the old gaff. Shows a bit of class, wouldn't you say?

JIM   Absolutely.

SEBASTIAN	They've an office in London. *(Vague.)* Or they're affiliated to an office in London, any-way…. Wouldn't you agree, Ossie, it's a good sign, them wanting to see me at five?
OSCAR	Five?
SEBASTIAN	Yeah, five … isn't that what they said? *(To* JIM*)* Oscar took the call. Didn't you, Oscar, take the call from them?
OSCAR	Who?
SEBASTIAN *(stands and begins towards* OSCAR*)*	The publishers for Christ's sake! I've to be there at five?
OSCAR	Oh yeah. The publishers. That's right. Five-ish, they said.

SEBASTIAN is *now beside* OSCAR. OSCAR *begins to move away.* SEBASTIAN *follows as he questions him.*

SEBASTIAN	Five-*ish*? I thought you said five?
OSCAR	Five. Five-ish. That's what your man on the phone said.
SEBASTIAN *(becoming more and more anxious)*	Jaysus, can you not answer a straight question?! Was it five or five-ish? Was the word *ish* used?
OSCAR	*Ish* isn't a word.

Now near the sofa, SEBASTIAN *grips him tightly by one shoulder.* JIM *stands up.*

OSCAR	Ow … owww! Around five, she said.

SEBASTIAN   I thought you said it was a he?

OSCAR   *She* was the secretary, the boss was a he. She
              handed the phone to he. Him. And *he* said,
              around five. How am I supposed to remember?
              I'm not a fuckin' answering machine, am I?

SEBASTIAN *(quietly)* I don't know what you are sometimes,
              Oscar.

> JIM *puts his good hand out, and firmly removes* SEBASTIAN*'s
> hand from* OSCAR.

SEBASTIAN *(almost pleading with* JIM*)* I need to know the exact....

JIM   What difference? *(He gestures at the snow.)* What
              difference can it possibly make now?

SEBASTIAN   I don't want them thinking I'm too eager by
              being on the dot, but at the same time....

OSCAR   Ah look, it was ages ago.

SEBASTIAN   It was eight days ago!

OSCAR   Well, I don't remember the exact....

SEBASTIAN   It was the day I was let go out of the job. *(To* JIM*)*
              Only clocked in when they gave me a cheque, told
              me grab a few suits and go home because they
              were locking the door and fucking off to Spain!
              (To OSCAR*)* My stomach was upset. I was in the
              jacks, and when I came out, you told me.... *I*
              remember anyway, because it took the sting out
              of the day. *(Beat.)* You said it was all meant to be
              ... the redundancy, the publishers ... coming at
              the same time. Providence, you called it.

OSCAR *moves back to the tree and resumes tying the dickie bows on it.* SEBASTIAN *follows him.*

OSCAR   Providence?

SEBASTIAN   We went to the bank to cash the cheque. First in the door we were. Then we went to celebrate. Eleven o'clock in the morning we hit the first pub. Half one the following morning we were still standing. Well, at a tilt…. Come on! We went to Hughes's and the Bachelor's and the Palace, and where did we not go? We met the man whose son had just got ten years for a hit and run. And, and, the schoolmaster who was on the mitch. And your man in Grogan's, used to be famous, what's his name? Jaysus, who did we not meet…? I gave you a loan of two grand for your college fees. Two fuckin' grand! Now you couldn't have forgotten *that!*

OSCAR   I don't say I forgot. I just say I don't recall the details.

Offstage, SEBASTIAN*'s mobile phone rings again.*

SEBASTIAN *(to* JIM*)* What time would you say it is now?

JIM   I told you, I don't know.

SEBASTIAN   What time does it get dark then?

JIM   About four … maybe.

SEBASTIAN   It's startin' to get dark now, isn't it? You can see the dark coming on. What time? Since the Angelus … how much?

JIM	I don't know, I told you already.
SEBASTIAN	Well, give a guess, can't you? At least do that!
OSCAR	Jaysus, Sebastian, you're like one of them Alzheimery people asking the time every minute. Will you give it a rest?
JIM	Quarter past ... maybe quarter *to*....
SEBASTIAN	What? Three? Yeah, three I'd say. That still leaves ... *(almost to himself, very agitated)* ... and another hour to reach....
JIM	You can't possibly think you are going *anywhere* in that....

SEBASTIAN*'s mobile phone rings again.*

SEBASTIAN *(shouts towards the door)* Ahhh, shut the fuck up, willya? I can't fuckin' answerya! Can I?!

Short pause as they all look at each other.

SEBASTIAN *(looks out the window, quiet)* If I've to *craaaawl* through that....

Sound of text message coming in.

SEBASTIAN	Fuck. What am I goin' to do? I can't think. Do you know why? I need a piss. I could, if I....

SEBASTIAN *pushes* OSCAR *out of the way and rushes into the kitchenette.*

OSCAR	The jacks is locked. Ah, not the sink. Jesus, not the....

SEBASTIAN   I'll wash it after me.

The sound of him pissing into the sink goes on for a good few seconds. OSCAR and JIM listen, occasionally glancing at each other. OSCAR is visibly disgusted, and sits on the sofa. After a moment he picks the box up and looks inside, then he pulls the rabbit out and cradles it against his belly.

SEBASTIAN *(from the kitchen)* Christ, the relief. The sweet, sweet relief. *(The sound of him trying to turn on the tap.)* Eh, it seems the water is gone off. The pipes must be…

OSCAR   Ah, for Christ's … *(disgusted)* that's just….

SEBASTIAN   How was I to know?

JIM *picks up the water bottle, sees that it's empty and drops it.*

OSCAR   Why don't you have a shite in there while you're at it? *Really* show us what you're made of.

SEBASTIAN *comes back in, somewhat shamefaced.*

OSCAR   This is just great, this is. No party. No food. No water. No heat. No smokes. No nothin'. But hey, we do have the aroma of beer-infused piss waftin' in from the kitchen!

SEBASTIAN   Ah, shut up, you fussy little bastard.

SEBASTIAN *sits on the sofa beside OSCAR, who gets up and walks away, moving over to stand beside JIM.*

SEBASTIAN   Gimme back me rabbit so if you're gonna be like that.

OSCAR	He's keeping me belly warm.
SEBASTIAN	Give him to me now. I want him here.
OSCAR	I'm freezin'….
SEBASTIAN	Right, five minutes. But I want him back then. *(He contemplates the room.)* What about smashing the window?
OSCAR	It's iron-barred, head to toe.
SEBASTIAN	One of us could squeeze between them.
OSCAR	Well it ain't gonna be *this* one of us, if that's what you're thinking.
SEBASTIAN	You're the only one small enough to fit.
OSCAR	Jaysus, I'm not the fuckin' rubber man.
SEBASTIAN	You can try.
JIM	He won't fit.
SEBASTIAN	We might be able to squeeze him through.
JIM	Yeah, if we screw his head off first.
OSCAR	We *could* smash the window, I suppose, and shout through it.
JIM *(large)*	And who will hear us, Oscar?

SEBASTIAN *goes to the bedroom door and tries to force it with his shoulder. He comes back and takes a run at it. The door won't budge.*

SEBASTIAN *(sits on the sofa, breathless)* What the fuck? What the…? It's like the door is made of….

JIM   Steel?

SEBASTIAN *(feeling the cold now)* Yeah, Steel. Even if he comes this second, I'm not going make it, am I?

(Beat.)

OSCAR *(stands)*   Would there be, you know, someone in the house?

SEBASTIAN   Nah, we'd know, wouldn't we? Look, there has to be an explanation. Maybe the locks are frozen. Or, or … there's an automatic security system, somethin' like that. We could've triggered….

JIM   It's getting so dark now.

OSCAR *goes to the light switch, and clicks it on a few times.*

OSCAR   There's no electricity.

SEBASTIAN   What? Fuck off! Fuck *off.*

OSCAR   No.

SEBASTIAN *goes around the room trying out light switches. When he gets to the mirror, he pulls the cord and this time the light over the mirror goes on. He is hugely relieved. He stays and looks for a moment into the mirror. Finding his own reflection disturbing, he turns away.*

OSCAR *(worried)* Let's just get out of here. I don't care how, just let's. Break the door down, Sebastian. Why can't you just break the door down?

SEBASTIAN   I can't. I've tried.

OSCAR *(more worried)* You can. You're not trying hard enough. You never try hard enough.

SEBASTIAN   I have tried. I *did* try. Jesus. All right, all right, I'll try again. Jim, come over here. At the count of three, I'll shoulder it from this side, you from the other.

JIM stands, as if preparing himself.

OSCAR   No!

SEBASTIAN   There's nothing else we can do.

OSCAR   He can't.

SEBASTIAN   What the fuck are you talking about now, you moron. Jesus, how I ever allowed myself get lumbered with you....

Beat, while OSCAR feels the sting of that remark.

OSCAR   He can't go rushing at the door. Not with his hand.

SEBASTIAN   What's wrong with his hand?

OSCAR   It's sprained. Yeah. Last night. Trying to stop the fight *you* started.

JIM, caught off guard, takes a few steps back.

SEBASTIAN *(to JIM)* What's he...?

JIM *(shifty)*   It's ... it's nothing really. I got caught up in the....

OSCAR   It is in its bollix nothin'! He had to go to the
                 hospital.

JIM   An accident. Nobody's fault.

OSCAR *(childishly triumphant)* He can't play his concert. Hope
                 you're happy now. Show him, Jim. Go on,
                 show him.

JIM   I told you I wanted no big deal made....

SEBASTIAN   Show me.

   JIM *lifts his hand to show it, then puts it down again.*

SEBASTIAN   Show again....

   JIM *lifts his hand for a little longer this time. Angelus bells ring.*

SEBASTIAN   Is that...?

OSCAR   Six o' clock.

SEBASTIAN *(quietly raging)* Shit. Fuck it. Just fuck it....

SEBASTIAN *sits at desk as lights go out.*

End of scene.

Scene 5

Some time later.
Lights go up (dusk-dim).

JIM *stands, facing the room near the window.* SEBASTIAN, *face turned into the back of the sofa, is fast asleep, occasionally snoring, covered in newspapers. The sound of splashing from the kitchen, then* OSCAR *comes out, sheepishly pulling up his fly. He pauses at the counter. He is shivering and appears to be unwell.*

JIM   Did you sleep?

OSCAR   Yeah, a bit. You?

JIM (*notices* OSCAR*'s condition, and begins to take off his coat*) Here, take this.

OSCAR   Ahh, no thanks, you're a-a-all right….

JIM   Go on. Take the bloody thing!

    OSCAR *takes the coat and begins to put it on.*

JIM (*settles the collar on* OSCAR*)* Oscar? Do you have the keys? You can tell me.

OSCAR   No, I don't fuckin' have them! Why would you
                 even think that?

JIM   To keep us here maybe.

OSCAR   What are you talkin' about?

JIM   To stop me from leaving. To stop your brother
                 from seeing the publishers. Out of jealousy. I
                 know you are jealous of him.

OSCAR   Well, let me tell you now, you are way off the
                 mark.

JIM   You're not jealous?

OSCAR   I don't have the keys. If I had the keys, I'd be
                 gone. You don't think I'd still be…. Jesus. Look
                 at it.

JIM *(quiet and slow)* Yes. Of course. Yes. *(Rubs his fist into his forehead.)*

OSCAR   Look, it'll be fine, Jim. Lofty will know
                 something is up. Don't you think, Jim? No
                 answer from the phone. No phone call from
                 Sebastian. He'll know…. He's not stupid.
                 And the party people will come. Some peo-
                 ple only go to a party after the pubs close
                 – don't they? Would you say the pubs are
                 closed yet?

JIM   I don't know. Maybe.

OSCAR   Jesus, what's this made of, c-c-concrete?

JIM   My father's.

OSCAR	Ah ... I don't want w-wearin your d-d-dead d-da's coat, thanks v-very much *(goes to take the coat off)*.
JIM	Keep it on, won't you? Stay warm.
OSCAR	Yeah, okay. T-t-ta.
JIM	Same age as me, that coat.
OSCAR	Yeah?
JIM	Bought in Germany. The day I was born.
OSCAR	I thought you said you were born here...?
JIM	Oh, *I* wasn't there, he was. The school I went to? He used to work there. A *Musik-Gymnasium* they call it.
OSCAR	*Musik-Gymnasium?* Sounds fun.
JIM	Yeah, doesn't it? *(Short, bitter laugh.)*
OSCAR	So he was a musician then?
JIM	No, a music teacher.
OSCAR	Same thing?
JIM *(definite)*	No. *(Beat.)* He was the choirmaster. Used to arrange music for it, write it sometimes, all that.... But ... but what he was really good at was prepping the boys for competitions. Yes, he excelled that way. He'd give you his spiel and.... Should have been a boxing coach really. *(He clenches his fist, and hits a branch of the tree.)*

73

OSCAR   Sounds a bit like my mother. Education, that'd
               been her thing. Now *she* should a been a Jesuit.
               Nose to the grindstone all the way. Hold it
               down for you too if you tried comin' up for....

OSCAR *sees that* JIM *isn't listening and relents.* JIM *stands at
the tree, hanging things he's found from the toy box and looking at
toys (wind-up snow ball).*

JIM   The day I was born it was snowing ... *(beat)* and
               he walked over the fields to the village station
               and took the train into Westerhausen, where he
               bought that coat. Probably the most money he
               ever spent on himself. To spend money, you
               see ... it was almost as if it hurt his feelings.

OSCAR *sits on the armchair and listens attentively.*

OSCAR   What, like, he was a miser?

JIM   He was saving up for something. It blinkered
               him.

OSCAR   What was that?

JIM   Me.... Well, my career really. Every penny went
               towards it. Private classes, decent piano, cotton
               wool to wrap me up in. This is *before* I even went
               to the school. I used to think it was a thing, some-
               thing to hold in your hands. Yim's career!

OSCAR   'Yim'?

JIM   Yim. He was Russian, my father. You didn't
               know that, of course. Why would you? I go by
               my mother's name.

OSCAR   Why do you do that?

JIM   It seemed like a good idea after I came back
               here. I thought it would make things simpler. I
               could stop always having to explain myself, to
               feel like I was trying to blag my way into some
               private club. The Irish, in case you don't know,
               think very highly of themselves. And no one
               can spell the fucking thing anyway.

OSCAR   Half-Russian, wha'? So how long before he saw
               you then?

JIM   Two, maybe three years. Oh, I'm not complain-
               ing, I was only a baby, what the fuck did I care?

OSCAR   Yeah, but, still … you know?

JIM   Besides, he made up for it later. Oh yeah, he
               did that all right. But I must tell you, he did
               have a photo sent over.

OSCAR *(uncertain)* So he knew what you … at least … I suppose
               … looked like…?

JIM   Oh, the photo wasn't of *me*. Well, not much
               of me, anyhow *(half-laughing)*. Listen, this is
               very funny. He asked my mother to take a pho-
               tograph … of my hands, and post it to him
               (laugh fades). I found it in his room after he
               died, stashed between these old music sheets.
               All mottled with age. The only family picture
               he kept, by the way. These two little hands. It
               took a while to figure out what they were. Like
               something you'd see at the bottom of a fish
               tank. Two little creatures with natures *all* of

their own. He was not, as my mother used to say, the full rouble.

A beat while JIM *lays his hand on the windowpane.*

OSCAR   Do you know, Jim … I don't think I ever heard you talking so much about yourself before. Talking so much about anything.…

JIM   What? Oh well. Why not? It makes no difference now *(turns abruptly to look at* OSCAR*)*. You know, they threw my father out of the school.

OSCAR   *What?* Like … sacked him?

JIM   Let's just say he was asked to leave.

OSCAR   But why?

JIM   On account of me. Too ambitious, you see. Pushing me always. Can you imagine that? Too ambitious for the Germans! *(Beat.)* My parents had long split by then. He stayed in Germany. Moved into digs in a village close to the school so he could be *neeeeaaaar* me. *(Beat.)* Light of my soul, that's what he called me. Russians, by the way, are *big* into the soul. Not the religious one of course, but the one you drag around with you, like a dying comrade on your back.

OSCAR *sees that* JIM *is becoming a little unhinged and starts to feel uncomfortable. He stands, and moves slightly away from the chair.*

JIM *(large)*   It's a game to the death, isn't it!?

OSCAR   What is?

JIM   All of it. Ahhh, fuck it, who *cares*? I don't. Do
             you?

    OSCAR, *feeling more uneasy, glances over at* SEBASTIAN.

OSCAR   Do you know, I feel a bit sick, Jim. I better lie
             down for a bit. Me head's on fire.

JIM *(mock surprise)* Is ... it ... really?

OSCAR   On fire. But me brain feels like a ... like a slab
             of ice cream or somethin'. I'll just lie down for
             a minute.

    OSCAR *goes to move towards the sofa.* JIM *grabs his sleeve.*

JIM   No. *Listen* to me. I want you to *listen*.

OSCAR   I am. I *will*. I just want to....

JIM   All day I've been listening to you, Oscar. On
             and on I've been listening to you. Now I'm try-
             ing *to explain* something here....

OSCAR   Okay, Jim, okay. Jesus....

    JIM *loosens his hold on* OSCAR*'s sleeve.*

JIM   The whole point of being there, you know.
             The whole point of every moment of every
             day was to train for competition. *(Beat.)* Until
             every fucking drop of music is *squeezed* out,
             and you have competed yourself dry.... And
             my old man ... *(beat).* On Sundays, other chil-
             dren were taken out of school for the day. I

would be nailed to the piano in his digs, locked into the room, and if I stopped, even for one minute stopped, he would come pounding down the stairs, then he would sit beside me and watch ... *(beat)*. An old brown banger in a tiny brown sitting room. And I had to play *and* play. And in between I had to listen *and* listen, to *him* ... telling me I must practise.

OSCAR   Jaysus, take it easy, Jim. You're a bit.... We're all a bit....

JIM   And pract*iiise* ... *(bitter)*. Oh, and how I'd have to beat all the other little fuckers too while I was at it, and keep beating them, year after year. Because *of course*, it would all be worthwhile in the end. And I believed him, you see. I believed him.

OSCAR   Ah, come on, Jim, now, it can't have been that bad. There must have been some bit of crack. What about friends...?

JIM   *Friends?* Don't make me laugh.... Ah, I think friendship is overrated anyhow.

OSCAR   Jaysus, thanks very much.

JIM   Mostly I don't remember ... *(beat)*. There was ... one boy, though. A soft boy. My father wrote a song for him once. Made him sing it over and over, until he got it right. *Weider. Weider. Und weider. Noch einmal.* Your patriot snowman reminded me. Do you know, he was the only person I've ever met who *literally* suffered from homesickness, cried so much he'd actually puke. His mother used to send him treats. You know, cake, toys, sweet things in a box. He would give it all away. Keep nothing. Everyone thought he was so generous. But of course, he wasn't generous at all. He was getting rid of it. Couldn't bear to be reminded. You know? In the end....

OSCAR   What?

JIM   He was carted off. Carted off to a mental home for children. Can you imagine? Two hundred and thirty-two lunatic children? Behind these big grey walls. Little bits of glass like *teeth* around the edges. *(He shows his teeth. Beat.)* This soft boy.

OSCAR   Jesus, why?

JIM   Oh, some sort of a breakdown. Well, you know how that is.

OSCAR   No, I don't! I got a bit exhausted once from too much studying, that's all. Over ... over-wrung ... and ... and that.

JIM   Okay. Fine. Anyway ... *he* ... he got this idea into his head that if he got frostbite in his hands he ... he couldn't play any more. He would be sent home. Didn't care if he lost his fingers. Just wanted out. And so, in the middle of the night, he got up ... and started to make snowmen.

OSCAR   Snowmen?

JIM   Yeah ... small ones. Only about this high *(a foot or so)*. All night he stayed up. By dawn there was this army of dwarf snowmen all over the back quad and he screaming at them and crying and bashing their heads off with his shovel.

SEBASTIAN *wakes up and begins to turn around. The others don't see him.*

OSCAR   Poor little bastard.

JIM   He must have been down there for hours, half the school watching him from the dormitory windows.

OSCAR   Why did no one stop him?

JIM   Watching him in silence. *(Beat.)* You know, I used to wonder about that, why somebody didn't wake a teacher? Of course I know now. So easy to know *now*. Competition, you see. One less to worry about.

OSCAR   I really feel rotten. My head, it's….

JIM   Hot. Brain cold. I know, I know. You're a baked Alaska.

SEBASTIAN *begins to sit up.*

OSCAR   Sorry. It's just … I keep thinkin', I keep thinkin'.

JIM   That we're trapped?

OSCAR   No … no. We're not trapped. Are we?

JIM   Can we get out?

OSCAR   I keep thinking….

JIM   That we will die in here?

OSCAR   No … *no.*

JIM   Do you know what I kept thinking today, every
             time I looked out the window?

OSCAR   What?

JIM   I kept thinking, there is my father, walking
             away, no coat, in the snow.

OSCAR   No … oh Jesus. *(He goes to take the coat off.)*

JIM *(low and cold)* Leave it on, I'm telling you. Leave it.

> OSCAR *goes to move away and* JIM *stops him, holding his upper
> arm.* SEBASTIAN *gets ready to stand up.*

JIM   Your brother…. Your brother will tell you
             something soon. Something he heard last
             night….

OSCAR *(very nervous)* Ah, I don't mind anythin' that fella says; you
             should know that….

> JIM *grabs his other arm using his bandaged hand.*

JIM   Oscar, will you listen to me?

OSCAR   That hurts … Jesus, Jim, let go, willya?

JIM   I'm only trying to tell you, I'm only….

OSCAR   It's too late to tell me anything. *(Beat.)* Lofty is a
             selfish bollix. There's no way he'd come out in
             that. And even if he wanted to, he'd never get

down that lane. And as for the party? It's the middle of the night, no one's comin'. Maybe no one was ever gonna come, snow or no snow. I don't know how we're going get out. Do you know? I think it's too fuckin' late, Jim.

JIM (*holding both of* OSCAR's *hands*) Now you're getting it, Oscar. Now you're finally getting it. Are you afraid? I am. I'm afraid. I shouldn't have come back here. Why the *fuck* did I ever come back here?

SEBASTIAN (*quiet but firm*) Let go of him now.

JIM *is still holding onto* OSCAR's *arm. They look at each other.*

SEBASTIAN   Let go now, I'm warnin' you.

JIM (*sadly*)   I was only trying to tell you. I was only trying to explain.

JIM *lets go of* OSCAR's *arm with a small, slight push.*

End of scene

Scene 6

Some time later.

Banging sounds. Lights go up, almost dark, but just enough light to see by.
SEBASTIAN *is running around, muttering about his rabbit, searching, gasping.*
JIM *is dozing on the sofa.* OSCAR *is on the floor, resting his head on his knees.*
The toy box is lying on its side near the sofa, empty.

SEBASTIAN   Where's? Where's me...? *(He searches around the sofa.)* The rabbit? Oscar, me rabbit's gone.

OSCAR *(looks at him, beginning to come round)* Wha'?

SEBASTIAN   When I fell asleep he was right here.... Right *here,* lying on me chest *(presses two hands to his chest).* He can't just have disappeared! *(Looks under the sofa.)*

JIM   Unless he is a magician's rabbit...?

SEBASTIAN *(angry)* Did I ask you...?

OSCAR *(begins to get up)* Here, we'll give you a hand looking for....

SEBASTIAN (*raises a warning finger to* JIM) You stay there. You just *stay.*

OSCAR   Okay, *I'll* help then.

SEBASTIAN   I should have stayed awake. I should have minded him. (*A beat while he hunts for the rabbit.*) But I couldn't keep me eyes opened, could I? Didn't get a wink last night, did I? With him. With him banging on his piano.

JIM   I wasn't....

SEBASTIAN (*large*) Well somebody was!

JIM (*worried*) *gets off the armchair and stands behind it.*

SEBASTIAN   I wouldn't mind, but we had to have the *singing* as well! Singing in this stupid squealy voice....

JIM   You heard that too?

OSCAR (*fixes on* JIM) Jim?

SEBASTIAN   Ah, look! There he is (*edges up on his knees to the far end of the sofa*). There, stuck right in the corner. Come on, Rabbit. Come here to me now, come on me bunny bun ... ow! (*He jumps back and sits on his heels.*) He *bit* me. (*He puts his hand in his mouth and sucks.*) Je-sus. (*Hurt.*) What he do that for?

JIM   You cornered him.

SEBASTIAN   He's after bitin' me, and I only tryin' to....

JIM   He is doing the only thing that he can do.

SEBASTIAN *(getting to his feet, angry, nervous)* Did I fuckin' ask you? *(Beat.)* He's hungry, that's all. Now I don't want to hear another word outta you till we're out of here.

JIM   Till we're what?! *(Short laugh.)* Oh, Sebastian!

SEBASTIAN *goes to the counter where* OSCAR *has left the plastic wrapper with a few bits of bread still in it.*

OSCAR *(moving to stand beside* JIM*)* You're lying about the piano. Why are you lying about the…?

JIM   How many times?!

SEBASTIAN   Course he is, you fuckin' moron! The piano, and the rest of it.

OSCAR, *puzzled, looks at* SEBASTIAN.

SEBASTIAN   His *hand*, Oscar, there's fuck all wrong with his hand.

OSCAR   Your hand?

SEBASTIAN   No nurse ever bandaged that hand. And if she did, she oughta be sacked.

OSCAR   Your hand, Jim?

SEBASTIAN   He wasn't anywhere near me when that fight broke out, when that fight finished, or any time in between.

OSCAR   I'm not asking you, Sebastian. I'm asking *him*.

SEBASTIAN   I saw him. On the far side of the bar, sitting up on the counter with that beardy oul' lad standing right behind him. I saw them both through the mirror.

JIM *(startled)*   What beardy oldfella?

SEBASTIAN   Oh, come on!

OSCAR   Is that true? Jim? Answer me!

JIM   What? Yes. *Yes*, all right, he saw me. He saw *me!* But I was on my own. *(To* SEBASTIAN.*)* Describe him. Describe the beardy oldfella.

OSCAR   But your hand, Jim?

SEBASTIAN   You bottled out of your concert and thought you'd take a dump on me. Let everyone think that I, *I*, destroyed your big chance. Coward.

JIM   That's not how it was.

SEBASTIAN *(angry)* You hadn't the balls to go through with it, so you decided....

JIM *disturbed, rubs his face with his bandaged hand.*

OSCAR *(large, angry)* I'm asking *him*. *(Quiet.)* I'm askin' you, Jim. If you didn't want to play, why didn't you just say? All you had to do was just say....

JIM *shakes his head, starts laughing bitterly, and tries not to.*

OSCAR *(disappointed)* Ah, Jesus now, Jim....

JIM *(stops laughing)* It wasn't a concert. It was a competition. I wasn't even going to mention it. I just wanted to quietly enter it. Nobody would need to know. But you were all the time at me to do something about my *career*, and I ended up telling you it was a concert just to shut you up….

OSCAR *Me?* You're gonna blame me now, is that it?

JIM All the time at me. Standing behind me in pubs, at parties. *'My friend the concert pianist. You have to hear him playing! Some day he'll be. Hey girls, have you met? My friend the piano man …'.* Pushing. Shoving. Standing behind me. Well it's not the same, Oscar. Banging out a few tunes at a party when you're drunk? It's not the same as a fucking competition. I only wanted to find my nerve again.

OSCAR I wasn't pushing. *(He begins to get upset, his voice tightening.)* I was just proud of you, that's all.

JIM But it's not your business to be *proud* of me, Oscar. I'm nothing to you. You are nothing to me. *(Beat.)* I didn't lie about playing last night; I swear that much to you.

OSCAR But I heard it, Jim. Sebastian heard it. The singing!

JIM Not from me. I wasn't singing. Oh Jesus… *(quietly afraid).*

OSCAR Did you lock the doors?

JIM Did *you?*

SEBASTIAN   Why would he?

JIM   To keep us here. To stop me from leaving. I told him I was leaving. To stop you from meeting the publisher. Who knows? He is jealous. He is also needy. Think about it, Sebastian.

SEBASTIAN *glares at* OSCAR *as if considering the possibility.*

OSCAR *(keeps his eyes on* JIM, *and gives a short, bitter laugh)* What did it sound like, Sebastian? The song. Can you remember, how did it go?

SEBASTIAN *(shrugs, uncertain)* Just, you know ... notes, a voice. A ... a sort of hymn thing.

OSCAR, *still looking at* JIM, *sings a few bars from* **Snowfall** (song).

SEBASTIAN   That's it, that's the one. *(He begins vaguely to join in.)*

JIM *then joins in. His singing is bitter, angry, a little unhinged. After a few notes, the other two stop singing, and he continues alone for a bar or so.*

JIM   I know you heard it. I know Sebastian heard it. I heard it too, but I thought it was all in my head. I'm hearing it now. It's him.

OSCAR   Who? Who are you talking about?

JIM   Oscar, there is no piano in that room. I tried to cancel, but my phone ... you know this. Because the moment I came into this house, I knew. I just *felt*.... Ah, fuck it. What does it matter now whether you believe me or not? *(Beat.)*

SEBASTIAN *(moves to the sofa and sits down)* You must think now that we're a right pair of … Oscar, get over here.

JIM   Lorraine … what did she tell you?

SEBASTIAN   Nothin'. I'm not discussing it. Oscar!

OSCAR is mulling things over, disturbed, but more angry than afraid.

JIM   She told you my father was dead anyway? She told you that much?

SEBASTIAN   She told me that much. *Oscar?*

JIM   What did he look like? The man with the beard. Describe him. Just describe him, can't you, for fuck's sake!

SEBASTIAN   I don't know. Thin. Wet beard down to his belly button. Trousers soaked up to the knee as if he'd waded to the pub. A tramp, I suppose. Look, you saw him yourself, stop trying to change the subject!

JIM   But that's the thing, I didn't see him.

OSCAR *(to* JIM) You're a liar. You're a fucking liar.

SEBASTIAN   Get over here. *Now,* Oscar!

OSCAR *(quick glance at* SEBASTIAN) *What?* What do you want?

SEBASTIAN   I'm tellin' you, get over here now.

OSCAR   Look at you, all delighted with yourself, aren't you? Delighted you caught him out. To be the one to tell me about his hand.

SEBASTIAN   But sure you must have noticed, Oscar. He had you gripped by it, Oscar *(makes a gesture referring to a few moments earlier).*

JIM   Maybe he didn't want to notice.

SEBASTIAN   Oscar…? Ossie? Come on now.

OSCAR   What's the matter? Afraid over there on your own, are you? Afraid of the dark? Is that it? You're afraid of the … *(laughs).*

SEBASTIAN   Don't be so….

OSCAR   Or is it *him?* You're afraid of *him?* Or the beardy oulfella maybe? Do you think he's comin' to get you? Woo-oo….

SEBASTIAN   I just want you to stay away from him. That's all.

JIM *(makes a move)* Look…. I'll go into the kitchen.

SEBASTIAN   You stay where I can see you. All the time see you, Oscar!

OSCAR   No!

    JIM *shoves* OSCAR *across the room*

JIM   Ah, get over to him then. The sight of you. The *soooouuund* of you. Go on. Get away from me. For fuck's sake, you make me sick.

    OSCAR *stumbles, falls on the ground, then turns, hurt, and looks at* JIM. *He then pulls himself to his feet.*
    SEBASTIAN *picks up the bag with crumbs of bread in it and steps back to the sofa.*

SEBASTIAN   Taking his side over mine, haw? I mean, forget
                   for a minute what he did or didn't do. And *you*,
                   by the way, don't know … the half of it.

JIM *(large)*   Well, why don't you *tell* him then? Just *(quiet)* tell
                   him?

SEBASTIAN *makes a small move towards* JIM.
JIM *looks steadily at him, unafraid.* SEBASTIAN *backs down,
turns, and kneels at the sofa, tempting the rabbit with a bit of
bread.*

SEBASTIAN   Come on. I'm not gonna hurt you *(makes tut-
                   tut rabbity noises)*. *(To* OSCAR*)* If I tell you get
                   away from someone, it's because I'm lookin'
                   out for you. Don't I always look out for you.
                   Haw?

OSCAR *stands staring at* SEBASTIAN*'s back. We can see the
resentment build.*

SEBASTIAN   I'm your brother. Your *brother.*

OSCAR   I'm sick of you calling me names.

SEBASTIAN   Ah, would you ever….

OSCAR   I'm sick of you calling me *names.*

OSCAR *walks away from him, opens the kitchen door and steps
inside. When* SEBASTIAN *begins to speak, he turns, stops, and
comes back and stands in the doorway.*

SEBASTIAN   But sure what does it matter what I call you,
                   Oscar? You're my intellectual superior anyway,
                   isn't that so? That's always been understood.
                   And why? Because you went to college and I

didn't? Fuck knows you did that all right. How many's that now? With your year of this, a couple of months of that, a half-arsed degree in the other. Oh yeah, Mammy thinks he'd make a good lawyer on account of his *contrary* disposition, and so he picks law. Fuck's sake, law! The boredom of it! Wouldn't touch it if you paid me….

OSCAR   Just as well, seeing as how you got about four points in your leaving cert.

SEBASTIAN   I didn't need to do well. Not with the job I have.

OSCAR   You haven't got a job.

SEBASTIAN   Jealous is all you are.

OSCAR   Of what, exactly? Your inside-leg-measuring skills?

SEBASTIAN *bends to the rabbit hiding under the sofa.*
OSCAR *is positioned close to the open doorway of the kitchen.*

SEBASTIAN   Afraid now I'll be gettin' a bit of attention, is that it? Is that what's stuck up your ho…?

Under the sofa, the rabbit makes a sudden dart and runs through the door into the kitchen. OSCAR *sees it coming and rushes in after it.* SEBASTIAN *lunges, but falls flat on his face. The door closes over as he lies there cursing.*

SEBASTIAN   Get away from my rabbit. Give him back, ya fuckin' bastard. My rabbit.

Door opens, and OSCAR *comes out with the (real) rabbit in his arms. He steps over* SEBASTIAN*, and comes Centre Stage.*

The row will slowly build: at first quiet and vicious.
N.B. It is important to note that any one of the three is capable
of hurting the rabbit.

SEBASTIAN   Give him to me.

OSCAR   No.

SEBASTIAN *(getting to his feet)* Give him back here.

OSCAR   No way I said.

SEBASTIAN   You only want him because he's mine.

OSCAR   Well, he's mine *now*.

SEBASTIAN *(standing)* So fuckin' smart, aren't you?

OSCAR   Am I?

SEBASTIAN   He's right, isn't he? You locked the doors to
keep me from the publishers. You jealous....

OSCAR *(amused)* He's not, you know.

SEBASTIAN   So fuckin' clever. And what is it you're studying now anyway, Oscar? Oh, wait now, I have
it. Human Resources. What is that anyway?
Sounds like something invented by the Nazis.
Ah, don't bother explaining. Next week it'll be
somethin' else. Like, no rush, Oscar, you're
only 30.

OSCAR   And what have you done since leaving school?
What have you achieved to make you so fuckin'
great? You don't even have a job now. You'll
probably never have one again.

SEBASTIAN   Fuck you. I'm a writer.

OSCAR   And what makes you think you're a writer? Like, who told you that? Who told you you were a writer?

SEBASTIAN   Why else did the publishers want to see me?

OSCAR   And who told you they wanted to see you in the first place? Oh, that's right, it was *me*, wasn't it? But sure I made that up. And no, I didn't lock the doors to keep you from the publishers. Because there was no need. There were no publishers. No meeting. I made it all up.

SEBASTIAN   No you didn't.

OSCAR   Oh I did. Well no, in fairness. Not the whole thing. Rule number one of lying through your arse, have a framework of truth to hold up the lies. Was it you taught me that? So yes, they phoned all right. *She*, it was definitely a she. And a she with no interest whatsoever in publishing your crappy novel. In fact....

SEBASTIAN   Why didn't she just write to me then?

OSCAR   Now *that* I don't know. Because the others, and I'm not talking about the first five or six, they all emailed.

SEBASTIAN   The others?

OSCAR   I lost count in the end. Not one of them interested in your crappy novel anyway. Now why was that?

SEBASTIAN *(stops)* You read my emails?

OSCAR   Why wouldn't I read your emails? I was the subject of enough of them. Reporting back to Mammy on my every move, my every....

SEBASTIAN   You'd no right reading my emails!

OSCAR   I deleted the more hurtful ones to save your feelings. More than you ever did for me.

SEBASTIAN   Spite.

OSCAR   You think, yeah? But do you know the real reason she rang? Like, the fuckin' cheek of her, when I think of it. To offer you a place in her boyfriend's workshop. Yeah, a writing class for beginners. Eight hundred euro they were looking for. Like, talk about a scam. You can either write or you can't, isn't that what you do always say?

SEBASTIAN   You were always a spiteful little prick.

OSCAR *and* SEBASTIAN *face each other.* OSCAR *prods him in the chest while he says the following.* SEBASTIAN *steps backwards, deflated.*

OSCAR   Inner city gritty novel. Gritty city inner novel, nitty, bitty, shitty novel that's never gonna see light of day. Bitty, titty, city novel, where everyone is called by a serial number and there's relief booths on every corner where a social welfare token buys you a wank. Wishful thinking there, Sebastian.

SEBASTIAN   Fuck you.

OSCAR   And where it's all, *all* been done before, only
             with better writing. I'm not lying, Sebastian.
             You know I'm not.

SEBASTIAN *steps back and sits at his desk, stunned with dis-*
appointment.

OSCAR   Ahhh. Is that a tear I see there in your eye,
             Sebastian? Hard man feeling the punch of
             disappointment now? You're not a writer,
             Sebastian. You never were. *(Beat.)*

SEBASTIAN   But you always said … you said….

OSCAR   What, that you could write! That you had
             talent? You're a bully, Sebastian. I tell you what-
             ever you want to hear.

SEBASTIAN   You're lying!

OSCAR   Surprised you didn't cop it actually, and you so
             smart.

SEBASTIAN   All I've done for you….

OSCAR   Oh, here we go. Now who's sounding like an
             oul' one?

SEBASTIAN   I took it for you. All those years I looked out
             for you….

OSCAR *(steely)*   Nobody fuckin' asked you.

SEBASTIAN   *Mammy did!*

OSCAR *winces slightly.*

SEBASTIAN   I carried you, brought you places, introduced you to....

OSCAR   What? A few alcoholic arseholes who convince themselves they're artists so they never have to work? Stick them.

SEBASTIAN   You'd still be sitting on the sofa beside Mammy with your sweeties watching Saturday night telly, only for me. You don't think it's odd, Oscar, no? That you're supposed to be havin' a party? A 30th birthday party, and your phone's only rang the once? And that was probably Mammy to make sure you wiped your arse.

OSCAR   Be as bitchy as you like, still not gonna make you a writer.

A beat while SEBASTIAN *realises the disappointment.*

SEBASTIAN   I couldn't stop thinking about.... You let me *talk* about it. *(He struggles to control himself.)* I thought, for once, I don't know ... I could say ... fuck the lot of you, lookin' down your noses at me, my family. Look at me now. *I have worth. We have worth.* And you stamp all that out? Why? Because you were clever in school? Because for five years you never crossed the door, swottin' and sweatin' and ploddin' till you knew it *all* by *heart?* While I was sent out to do every scabby part-time job in the town? So we could pay for it? So fuckin' what, Oscar, if you were clever in school? So was half your class. So is half of everyone's class. *(Beat.)* Doesn't mean they're not gonna end up living in a kip like this, alone, owning nothin', having no one. I'm your *brother*, for fuck's sake. Your *brother.*

OSCAR *is positioned behind the sofa.* SEBASTIAN *approaches him from the other side.* OSCAR *softens, feels bad, and takes a step forward.* SEBASTIAN *stands and for a second it looks like they might be going to embrace.*

OSCAR *(apologetic)* Sebastian, I'm … I'm….

Then SEBASTIAN *lunges.*

SEBASTIAN   I'll fuckin' kill you. I'll puncture your fuckin' face.

SEBASTIAN *throws a punch at him.* OSCAR *doubles over (behind the sofa, where he puts the real rabbit in a box and pulls out the toy rabbit).* OSCAR *straightens up.*

SEBASTIAN   You might be cleverer, but you're not stronger. I'll tear your fuckin' head off.

OSCAR *and* SEBASTIAN *begin pulling the rabbit between them, the rabbit struggling as they pull. They curse and swear at each other and call each other names, in growls muffled with sobs.*

JIM   The rabbit! You'll kill the fucking rabbit!

OSCAR   Me fuckin' nose. You bust me nose! You bastard!

JIM   Jesus, Jesus, Jesus. *Christ*, will you…?

JIM *jumps up, lets out a roar of anger and frustration, ploughs in between them and grabs a hold of the rabbit. It gives a short final shudder. The three of them stop and stare down at it in* JIM's *hands.*

JIM   It's dead.

OSCAR   You killed it.

JIM   *You* killed it.

SEBASTIAN *(crying)* Me rabbit ... he's ... he's....

End of scene

Scene 7

Complete darkness.

OSCAR *and* SEBASTIAN *sit on the sofa,* OSCAR *huddled into the corner,* SEBASTIAN *sitting forward on the edge of it.* JIM *stands stock-still leaning against the wall behind them, eyes closed.*

The sound of whispers can be heard; echoing childlike whispers in English and German. 'Vo is mein papa? Where is my father? Vo is mein papa, my papa? Mein father?'

JIM   My father haunted me you know. Even when
               he was alive, he haunted me.

SEBASTIAN   Look, Jim … if you just … tell me where the
               keys are, I swear there'll be no more said. We'll
               go our separate ways and….

JIM *(weary)* How many times? I don't have the keys….
               (Beat) What were you asking me about? Oh yes,
               my father, the competition….

SEBASTIAN   I wasn't asking.

JIM   The final competition, you see, was the one
               that decided everything. What college, which

100

future. And he…. He was waiting for me on the steps of the concert hall for hours, waiting with his pinched face and clenched hands, hardly able to control himself. Other fathers had driven there, or travelled with their sons on school buses, but he had to walk through the fields, through the snow. He had to *suffer*. Light of my soul. So fucking needy. Like your brother there. *(Beat.)* The bottom of his trousers soaked. Beard frosted and only starting to thaw. How did Oscar put it? Like a wet, manky jumper hanging out of his chin.

OSCAR　　　　　Oh God….

SEBASTIAN　　　Just give me the keys.

JIM　　　　　　Even if I did have the keys, Sebastian, what good are they now? We are clamped into this place. Don't you know that? *(Beat.)* I was ashamed of him, a quivering bag of bones, held together by that fucking overcoat. Always as old as myself….

OSCAR *weakly tries to take the coat off, then gives up.*

JIM　　　　　　There's no point in freezing, Oscar. *Use* it. He really thought I could win, you know? He wanted it *so* much.

SEBASTIAN　　　Let's just leave it then. Sleep. Let's just … sleep.

JIM　　　　　　Sebastian, you've already been asleep for hours.

SEBASTIAN　　　Have I?

JIM	And so, in the front row of the audience, I sat with the other contenders, all watching each other, applauding each other, pretending we didn't want to break each other's fingers!
SEBASTIAN	Oscar? Oscar, are you all right?
JIM	The masters in the row just behind us. My father two rows back, so that when I turned even a fraction I could see him. He could instruct me with a look, an eyebrow lift, the twist of a lip. He could coach me.
SEBASTIAN	Oscar is very upset. For his sake, would you not just…?
JIM	Boys from all over the world. *(Beat.)* Funny thing: you never remember the boy, only the country they come from … and the style of playing, of course. *(Beat.)* Did she tell you I killed him?
SEBASTIAN	No, of course not.
JIM	Did she tell you he killed himself then?
SEBASTIAN	Yes, she said she'd heard something like that all right.
JIM	Blamed me I suppose?
SEBASTIAN	No, no … she'd heard something, that's all.
JIM	Hmmm. Latvia was first. Big, broad movements, fearless. Latvia was a big show-off. Thought more of himself than the music. No need to worry about Latvia. Next China.

All technique. Flawless technique, a lot of wrist ballet. A *flamboyant* player, as they say. Again, my father gave me the nod, no need to panic.

SEBASTIAN   Oh, for fuck's sake....

JIM   Now, now. *You* asked....

SEBASTIAN   I didn't ask. Why do you keep saying that? I didn't *ask!*

JIM   Sebastian, you did, with your swipes, and your dirty looks and your *innuendo.* For hours and hours, one way or another, you have been *asking,* and so now I'm telling ... *(Beat.)* Russia ... ha ... I ought to have known! Now I noticed *him.* The boy first. Scrawny, delicate-looking, and so fucking shabby. Talk about your shitty tuxedos...! *(Beat.)* The rest of us, we were all spruced up, brushed and inspected and polished. And inspected again. But this boy... *(Beat.)* His shoes. When I saw his *shoes,* not even polished, bashed down at the heel.... You know the expression 'down at heel'? Well, that was him. I hadn't seen such poverty since I'd left here when I was living in those flats.... His suit way too small for him, and the trousers too short. You could see his white, no, greyish, ankle socks. Skimpy things. And in winter in Germany, even the poor wear long woollen socks. There was a *hole* in one of them, the right one. A hole in his sock. I couldn't, just couldn't get over that. For fuck's sake! *(Beat.)* But you're probably wondering about his playing.

SEBASTIAN   Shut up, just please *(starts crying)* shut....

JIM   It took seconds to ... to realise that I wasn't
noticing his playing. I couldn't tell you one
thing about it. But the music.... I could *feel*
it. It just poured over me. Like liquid all
over me. As if the piano didn't exist. As if
he didn't exist. The music was coming from
somewhere else. *(Beat.)* I looked back at my
father, but couldn't catch his eye. He was ...
he was staring up at the boy. Probably wondering how a father could get such a boy.
Instead of ... this boy, this soft boy, who
was his son. And I could see that he knew
what I already knew ... the whole thing ...
the whole thing had been a complete waste
of time. *(Beat.)* A little fucker with a hole in
one sock, you know?

JIM *moves behind the sofa, where he stands looking down on*
OSCAR *and* SEBASTIAN. *The two brothers are huddled*
together.

SEBASTIAN   Oscar, say something will you? Stay connected
now. Climb up, come on, back up. One rung
at a time. Don't stay down there. Stay with
me....

Snowfall (song) *softly plays chorus vocals only (a boy treble's*
voice).

JIM   I dream about it sometimes. About being in
my father's digs. Trapped in the sweaty Frau's
little brown sitting room. And it's like being
trapped in a womb or something. And always
I'm convinced that the more I play, the *harder*
I play, the bigger I will grow, and then ... I'll
be able to burst out! And I do get bigger. But
(laughs) so does the room. And there I am,

banging away on the piano till my skin starts to split. And ... the walls and the ceiling getting further away. Each piece I play, further away.

A beat, the light dims, **Snowfall** (song) *plays louder, a child's voice singing with words in German.*

JIM   You asked, and so I'm telling you now.

Darkness. **Snowfall** (song) *plays out.*

THE END